# THE PEAK PERFORMING TEACHER

*This book is simply a reminder written through my filters, lenses, personal history, and stories. It is written without judgment. We are all in this together. I am every teacher's biggest fan. Though I didn't invent any of the concepts contained herein, I hope my take on them brings you the next level of the joy and satisfaction you desire and deserve.*

# THE PEAK PERFORMING TEACHER
## FIVE HABITS FOR SUCCESS

MIKE KUCZALA

FOR INFORMATION:

Corwin

A SAGE Companyy

2455 Teller Road

Thousand Oaks, California 91320

(800) 233-9936

www.corwin.com

SAGE Publications Ltd.

1 Oliver's Yard

55 City Road

London, EC1Y 1SP

United Kingdom

SAGE Publications India Pvt. Ltd.

B 1/I 1 Mohan Cooperative Industrial Area

Mathura Road, New Delhi 110 044

India

SAGE Publications Asia-Pacific Pte. Ltd.

18 Cross Street #10-10/11/12

China Square Central

Singapore 048423

President: Mike Soules

Associate Vice President and
    Editorial Director: Monica Eckman

Publisher: Jessica Allan

Content Development Editor:
    Mia Rodriguez

Editorial Intern: Ricardo Ramirez

Production Editor: Tori Mirsadjadi

Copy Editor: Michelle Ponce

Typesetter: Hurix Digital

Cover Designer: Scott Van Atta

Marketing Manager: Olivia Bartlett

Printed in the United States of America.

*Library of Congress Cataloging-in-Publication Data*

Names: Kuczala, Mike, author.

Title: The peak performing teacher : five habits for success / Mike Kuczala.

Description: Thousand Oaks, California : Corwin, a SAGE company [2022] | Includes bibliographical references and index.

Identifiers: LCCN 2021046569 | ISBN 9781071853252 (paperback) | ISBN 9781071853269 (epub) | ISBN 9781071853276 (epub) | ISBN 9781071853283 (ebook)

Subjects: LCSH: Effective teaching. | Teaching–Psychological aspects. | Teachers–Psychology. | Teachers–Job stress. | Stress management. | Well-being.

Classification: LCC LB1025.3 .K82 2022 | DDC 371.102–dc23/eng/20211203

LC record available at https://lccn.loc.gov/2021046569

This book is printed on acid-free paper.

22 23 24 25 26 10 9 8 7 6 5 4 3 2 1

# CONTENTS

# PREFACE

*Peak performance begins with your taking responsibility for your life and everything that happens to you.*

*Brian Tracy*

I started writing this book in 1998. Life has been writing the contents ever since. Way back then as a youngish teacher—a band director more specifically—I was already a student of peak performance and high-performing habits. I had to be. With almost two hundred junior high band members and a grueling after-school and weekend schedule including halftime performances, marching, concert and jazz festivals, evening rehearsals, and yearly trips to competitions, I was in front of my students, their families, and the community on a daily basis. My career was often on very public display. I certainly didn't do everything right, but I was determined to be the very best I could be. Not that I had peak performance mastered (I still don't), but I was a serious student of the game of life. I devoured anything I could get my hands on by some of the masters of motivation including Tony Robbins, Stephen Covey, Brian Tracy, and Jack Canfield. I read books, listened to tapes and CDs, and even went to live seminars. In fact, I wrote to Tony Robbins in 2000 asking, "What are you doing for teachers?" In my view, teachers needed his peak performance principles more than any other part of society because every day they teach, poke, prod, push, motivate, and care for our greatest natural resource—children. His people did respond with a kind letter wishing me good luck in my quest and sent a collection of his books to the school where I was teaching at the time. I was grateful and continued my journey. At times I would even bring up the idea of the peak performing teacher in different educational meetings and settings to very little interest. I sat on the idea but never let go of it. My career took a long and winding road, but I now realize it was all preparing me for this new endeavor. I am genuinely excited to have moved forward with it.

I've earned my wings, so to speak, in the education field. I was born into a family of teachers—one sister, both parents, three grandparents, and even an aunt. What did I do when it came time to find a life partner? I married a teacher! If there is something you've experienced in education, from the pains and sorrows to the joys and successes, I've most likely experienced something similar. I left my K–12 teaching career in 2003 to become a regional coordinator of instruction with an educational consulting company called Regional Training Center (RTC). RTC partners with colleges and universities to offer graduate coursework and master's degrees for educators. I'm now the academic director and supervise the instructional side of the business. In my eighteen years with RTC, I have taught and designed graduate coursework, maintained college partnerships, and overseen a cadre of about one hundred graduate instructors who facilitate the coursework that reaches thousands of teachers every year.

My role with RTC also gave rise to my own consulting career. Over the past decade and a half, I've designed five graduate courses that have been taught by dozens of graduate instructors, authored three books, and delivered professional development and keynotes all over the world, mostly on the benefits of physical activity in teaching and training. I'm not saying any of this to impress you! I come from a humble family and know my roots well. I'm telling you this because I have made a choice to live life at a certain level. I like the feeling of success and achievement. Much of it comes from trial and error, mistake-making, and rejection. But it also happens through recognizing the growth that failure brings. I have learned to view failure not as a punisher but as a teacher.

Between my family, life in public schools, and my leadership role with RTC, I have come to find there are certain things that, if done on a consistent basis, can raise your level of living and giving. Isn't that what we're all after? Continuing to strive to live a better life and give some of that away to make the lives of others, specifically our students, better? Don't we all wish to be the very best we can be for every student we teach and feel good doing it? Is there a way to make this wonderful profession you've chosen even more joyful and satisfying to experience? In *The Peak Performing Teacher: Five Habits for Success*, I offer my perspective on what those things are—the concepts that supercharge my own life and the lives of many others, from living the physical life and managing stress to creating momentum and practicing gratitude. It is my way of giving back to the profession I love in the most profound way possible. Selfishly, it is also fulfilling my need to continue creating momentum and finding purpose in my own life. My hope is that this book will show you the peak performance principles that serve me for you to be inspired and, more importantly, to be the inspiration you were meant to be for your students.

# ACKNOWLEDGMENTS

I give thanks to the following people:

Publisher Jessica Allan for her advice, guidance, and belief in this project.

Eric Savage for making such an impactful contribution in writing about gratitude in Chapter 4.

Matt Bergman, Jennifer Caputo, David Gusitsch, Chris Walker, Tracie Gunnufson, Andy Vasily, and Dr. Missy Widman for sharing their morning routines in Chapter 5.

Diana Ramsey for her vision, guidance, and tutelage throughout my career and for creating and sustaining Regional Training Center (RTC), an organization that changed my life.

All the motivational and life teachers who have influenced me over the past three decades including (and especially) Tony Robbins, Stephen Covey, Jack Canfield, Brendon Burchard, Jesse Itzler, and others too numerous to mention. If you are familiar with any of their work, you will notice some of their concepts and language in mine.

# ABOUT THE AUTHOR

 **Mike Kuczala** has delivered keynotes, given presentations, facilitated professional development, and taught graduate courses on four continents. His presentations, courses, books, and videos have reached more than 100,000 teachers, trainers, corporate executives, and parents. He is also the coauthor of the Corwin bestseller and Association of Educational Publishers' Distinguished Achievement Award nominated *The Kinesthetic Classroom: Teaching and Learning Through Movement*, a book and philosophy that has changed the view of teaching and learning around the world. Mike's second book, *Training in Motion: How to Use Movement to Create an Engaging and Effective Learning Environment*, was released in 2015 (AMACOM), and *Ready, Set, Go! The Kinesthetic Classroom 2.0* (Corwin) was released in the summer of 2017. President of Kuczala Consulting and academic director for the Regional Training Center (RTC), Mike has given standing-room-only presentations that have been experienced in such diverse settings as The Educational Collaborative for International Schools, the East Asia Regional Council of Schools, the Francis Marion University Center of Excellence to Prepare Teachers of Children of Poverty Summer Institute, the American Society for Training and Development, the Forum for Innovative Leadership, the Association for Supervision and Curriculum Development, and the Society for Health and Physical Educators.

A former American Fitness Professionals and Associates Certified Nutrition and Wellness Consultant and an expert in training, training design, and effective presentation, Mike has designed or codesigned, four of the most successful graduate courses in the history of the Regional Training Center (RTC). *Motivation: The Art and Science of Inspiring Classroom Success, Creating Health and Balance in Today's Classroom, The Kinesthetic Classroom: Teaching and Learning Through Movement, and The Kinesthetic Classroom II: Moving Across the Standards* are facilitated by a cadre of more than seventy trained graduate instructors who have taught thousands of teachers the key principles of instructional movement, motivation, and wellness.

Mike proudly and humbly comes from a family of educators including his wife, sister, both parents, and three grandparents. He earned his bachelor of arts in music from Kutztown University and master of music education from the University of Northern Colorado. Mike enjoyed a ten-year band and choral directing career in both Colorado and Pennsylvania. "I am the product of three generations of teachers. Education is what I love and do. It is always an honor and pleasure to work with both educators in helping them to become true instructional leaders and corporate executives and trainers in providing presentation skill and effectiveness. My background in education gave rise to my love of teaching, public speaking, curriculum and training design, and helping people create goals and live their dreams."

For more information, please visit www.mikekuczala.com and/or www.thepeak performingteacher.com.

# INTRODUCTION

*Above all things, reverence yourself.*

Pythagoras

An anonymous source once said, "If you put a small value upon yourself, rest assured that the world will not raise your price." I could not agree more, yet continuously watch people put their own life and well-being near the bottom of their personal to-do list. Doing so not only impacts the quality of their lives, but also the quality of what they can provide to others. The 2020-2021 school year was arguably the most difficult in the history of American education; the impact sometimes devastating. For your own sake, and the sake of your students and colleagues, it's time to reverse the damage. Satchel Paige said, "Don't look back, something might be gaining on you." If you haven't made it to the bottom of your to-do list, what is gaining is not pretty. Today, you can change all that.

Simply stated, the greatest gift is self-love. Whether you realize it or not, this gift impacts everything you do, every action you take, every conversation you have, and every person you meet. Often people put everything else ahead of their health, well-being, personal vision, and purpose only to be not as effective at life. We take care of our children, students, spouses, parents, employment, pets, finances, friendships, homes, cars, and lawns but often pay little mind to our own bodies, health, and personal journey. If you want to be more effective, loving, productive, and useful, you must begin by putting yourself at the top of the list.

The case for vision, gratefulness, and wellness in a purposeful life cannot be overstated. There is no denying that maintaining a high standard for our lives can seem overwhelming and that it is a daily practice, but once we raise our level of living, living raises us. I call it "getting on the front end of things," because usually we work from the back end, where everything is a bit more difficult; frankly, a lot more difficult. Once you put yourself first through the creation of new habits, life flows. What once seemed like a chore is accomplished with vigor. The end of the day no longer brings exhaustion but a rested, peaceful feeling of accomplishment and balance. More gets done, and less energy is expended. What used to be tiring is now energizing. What a relief. You can be on that track. It is a choice. Change your mind, change your life. The greatest gift is one of health, wellness, energy, and vitality that you give yourself. Move "you" to the top of the list right now, and everyone around you will say "thank you," especially your students.

*The Peak Performing Teacher: Five Habits for Success* is my way of sharing of not only what works for me but also what works for others who enjoy the benefits of a purposeful and grateful lifestyle. Hopefully, the concepts, stories, examples, and practical ideas will move you to make that one decision that will change your life. I am humbled to provide ideas that will help you:

- Understand the key relationship between the brain and body
- Take responsibility for your well-being
- Create a morning routine that will have you arrive in your classroom with energy and excitement
- Live more harmoniously through personal vision, ambition, and gratefulness
- Learn what belies stress and how to beat it (you might be surprised!)
- Enjoy the power of physical activity, and understand its place in your life
- Unleash motivation you didn't know you possess

At the end of your life, all you will have is the person you've become. Your fullest potential cannot be achieved if the needs of your mind and body are ignored. You are inherently well-equipped for every challenge that lies ahead. It is my wish that with a clear destination, a lighted path, and the proper tools for the trip, you will make your journey with eagerness and a fresh outlook. It is also my wish for this book to become a daily inspiration that will change your life forever.

## THE MOST IMPORTANT PIECE OF EQUIPMENT

When I give a keynote address, lead a professional development seminar, or teach a graduate course centered on wellness or motivation, I always begin by describing the characteristics of the single most important piece of equipment in creating a desired lifestyle. The great thing is that most people already have one in their home! If used properly, this tool has the power to transform, lift, and propel us to new heights. What is it? A mirror. In it, you will find your greatest advocate for personal growth, power, wellness, and vision. The source of your sense of self, intrinsic motivation, and your satisfaction with every aspect of your life will be staring back at you. Your ability to act paired with your capacity for making decisions is the single greatest resource for achieving the personal and professional life you desire. Only you can take responsibility for taking the path to optimal daily living. And that level of life is only possible through experiencing unlimited energy every day. Michael Jordan said,

*The game is my life. It demands loyalty and responsibility, and it gives me back fulfillment and peace.*

Conversely, life is your game. If you demand loyalty and responsibility to it through vision, wellness, and routine, I promise you fulfillment and peace.

## THE ABCs OF ACHIEVEMENT

Before you step foot on a treadmill, practice a new breathing technique, or set a goal, I would like to share with you what I call "The ABCs of Achievement." There are three sets of ABCs, each one leading to the next. The first points to the fact that no matter where we start, they are critical to a new beginning.

## ACCEPTANCE

Find comfort in both your flaws and highlights and with the point at which you start this journey. Remember that success is, in part, defined by self-acceptance.

*One must have the adventurous daring to accept oneself as a bundle of possibilities and undertake the most interesting game in the world, making the most of one's best.*

*Harry Emerson Fosdick*

## BEGIN

Take the first step, and list the reasons why you must start your journey today. What are the possibilities if you do? What are the consequences if you don't?

*A journey of a thousand miles begins with a single step.*

*Lao Tzu*

# REFLECTION

What are your reasons to begin this journey? List the possibilities of beginning the journey now and the consequences if you don't.

Write your response here:

........................................................................................................................

........................................................................................................................

........................................................................................................................

........................................................................................................................

........................................................................................................................

........................................................................................................................

........................................................................................................................

## CHANGE

Change your mental focus to a life fueled by passion and health each day. Prepare yourself for energy, vitality, and productivity!

*Change always comes bearing gifts.*

*Price Pritchett*

**Once you've given yourself permission to accept your person, begin your journey, and change your mental focus, the next set of ABCs is critical to reaching your goals.**

## ATTITUDE

Attitude will determine how successful you'll be in your quest for a healthy and balanced life. It's the critical difference between "making it" to the gym or "putting it off" until tomorrow. It determines where "you" end up on your list of things to do. Attitude is the most impactful of personal attributes in creating a contagious environment for success or a toxic recipe for failure.

*The greatest discovery of my generation is that a human being can alter his life by altering his attitude.*

William James

## 🔍 REFLECTION

What part of your attitude would you adjust to make this journey more fruitful?

Write your response here:

..........................................................................................................................................................

..........................................................................................................................................................

..........................................................................................................................................................

..........................................................................................................................................................

## BELIEF

Belief provides the heat that fuels your personal fire each day. It is critical that you believe you can achieve anything that has your focused passion including dynamic health, your personal vision, and enthusiasm that supports a life of your design.

*Keep your dreams alive. Understand to achieve anything requires faith and belief in yourself, vision, hard work, determination, and dedication. Remember all things are possible for those who believe.*

Gail Devers

## 🔍 REFLECTION

What is one belief that you would like to change that you know would improve your life? How would you change it?

Write your response here:

..........................................................................................................................................................

..........................................................................................................................................................

..........................................................................................................................................................

..........................................................................................................................................................

..........................................................................................................................................................

## COMMITMENT

Commitment becomes the daily energy that makes a life purposeful. The most amazing thing about committing to a new level of living is how it envelopes all your pursuits. When you feel well and your energy levels rise, what seems impossible becomes ordinary. Wellness becomes the driving force of your life, and commitment to it provides the backdrop.

> Desire is the key to motivation, but it's determination and commitment to an unrelenting pursuit of your own goals—a commitment to excellence—that will enable you to attain the success you seek.
>
> Mario Andretti

 REFLECTION

What is one thing that you think you'll need to commit to in order to improve your life's outcomes?

Write your response here:

..............................................................................................................................

..............................................................................................................................

..............................................................................................................................

..............................................................................................................................

Attitude, belief, and commitment are a crucial part of achievement; they make it possible, in a world filled with obstacles, to master the principles in this book. Once the second set of ABC priorities are in place, you will feel the enduring pleasure and benefit of the final three.

**Achievement** of your goals,

**Beauty** and inner radiance through your response to the world around you, and

**Clarity** of vision and purpose.

### How will you change the world?

## THE POWER OF "MUST"

Gladys was a graduate student in one of my wellness courses. She made a choice to apply the principles I've just described and those that will be discussed throughout this book. Not only did she lose more than 60 pounds, last I knew she had kept the weight off for more than a year. She got up at 4:30 a.m. every weekday, was at the gym by 5:00, and worked out for an hour. She dropped three dress sizes and no longer felt compelled to get on the scale. Armed with information, passion, and personal strength, Gladys simply got leverage on herself. Instead of finding reasons not to work out, not to eat in a healthful manner, and not manage her stress, she listed the reasons why she could no longer afford to ignore what ailed her. In other words, she got disturbed and used it to her advantage. Exercise, healthful eating, and a balanced lifestyle became a "must" for Gladys, and it transformed itself into a brand-new lifestyle; no longer work but rather a joyful habit. At twenty or thirty years of age this all sounds very plausible, but Gladys was forty-seven.

What was misguided became informed. What was informed became a dream. What was a dream became a vision. What was a vision became a goal. What was a goal became a must. What was a must became action. What was "some" day became now. Gladys's hopes and dreams were realized; her goals accomplished; her life transformed.

I don't share this with you because I expect you to be in the gym at 5:00 a.m. every morning. I can safely say that I am not and won't ever be. I simply want you to think about your own life and what needs to be changed. What "should" might become a "must"? It might be practicing stress reduction on a more regular basis or beginning a gratitude journal. It's a very personal reflection but one I'd ask you to think about as you move through the reading.

## **Find the mirror!**

# WHAT ARE YOUR HOPES, DREAMS, AND GOALS?

*The great end in life is not knowledge but action.*

Thomas Henry Huxley

Now it is up to you to make a simple decision to change your life and turn your "shoulds" into "musts." Set your intent, know your purpose, and begin. Your time for the to-do list is now. You hold this book in your hands because you are ready to put yourself, your life, and your health first. Your ability to act, one of our great human powers, will make it all possible. It comes down to having a vision and being determined; to cut away all other possibilities except the one that has your focus of being healthy, dynamic, and vibrant. You will see your life expand right in front of you!

*What lies behind us and what lies before us are tiny matters compared to what lies within us.*

Ralph Waldo Emerson

## A WORD ABOUT PAIN AND PLEASURE

First, the pleasure . . .

To begin my graduate course, *Motivation: The Art and Science of Inspiring Classroom Success*, I purposefully try to create an association of pleasure within the group. As participants arrive, they find their course workbook opened to display a quote by Bo Bennett, a personal development speaker and coach:

*Enthusiasm is excitement with inspiration, motivation, and a pinch of creativity.*

The class is then instructed to be prepared to answer "get to know you" questions such as teaching responsibilities, hobbies, and the most interesting place they've traveled to in the last two years. At this point, my only goal is to create a fun and engaging environment that produces a sense of pleasure and belonging. While most participants enjoy this first section, some find it stressful. We introduce ourselves to each other, find people with the same birthdays, get the names of three people taller or shorter and the same height as we are. We share things about ourselves with a partner using only our bodies, introduce ourselves in conjunction with making a silly face, toss balls for more introductions, and discover similar likes and dislikes. This work at the beginning of a course pays off handsomely as we do cooperative work throughout the term.

Participants are then asked to work individually to select a preferred quotation from a curated list. After they have had the opportunity to read and select a quote, they are put into groups of three or four to discuss quote selections and choose one that will represent the entire group so they can relate it (through a spokesperson) to reasons for taking the course and its relationship to training. We end this activity with a quote from Billy Graham:

*Hot heads and cold hearts never solved anything*

Finally, I ask participants to create a list of goals for the course. What do they want to take away? What do they hope to get out of the course, and so on? We reference this list throughout the course.

It's a carefully crafted course introduction to purposefully create pleasure and build relationships—a foundational building block in classroom success. The usual response is smiles, laughter, and favorability. An hour into the course, people are feeling good and so much less stressed about taking a graduate course!

Now for the pain . . .

All Regional Training Center graduate courses feature a research-based project to complete their requirements. With that in mind, participants are now asked to review the many options of Learning Extension Project Guidelines. This information is reviewed carefully—project options, style and formatting considerations, and deadlines. It takes a bit of time to go through the entire process. Almost instantly, body language changes, and the positive energy I so carefully crafted leaves the room, which is perfect for this activity. After fielding questions, I hit participants with this question:

Will you be staying for the duration of the course?

This gets us to the point of the opening activity and highlights the fact that participants have been involved with learning on many levels since they entered the room. Most look at me like I'm crazy and answer "yes, of course." I repeat the question a time or two, ask "why," and chart the answers. I also ask about their feelings when they arrived and after the initial activities versus after the class discussion of the Learning Extension Project. Did they associate more pleasure with the course after the opening activities; more pain after they learned of the project requirements? It's normal to get answers such as "fun" and "pleasure" about the opening activities and "painful" and "unpleasant" with regard to the Learning Extension Project. My job is to lead them to these conclusions. I then ask, *"why did you stay?"* The following are some of the normal answers I receive:

I'm working on my master's degree.

I'm working on a certification or state requirements.

I'll get a raise.

I want to learn how to motivate myself and my kids.

I want to learn to be a better goal setter.

Now, a more interesting question. "What if the project requirement had been a fifty-page research paper? Would you have stayed?" The answer is often "no." What wins out—*pain or pleasure?*

I point out that for most of them the pain of leaving the course is greater than the pleasure of not taking the course; that the pleasure of receiving a pay raise by moving up on the salary guide is greater than the pain of not getting the raise. That the pain of not completing certification or master's degree requirements is greater than the pleasure of leaving or not having taken the course at all. This is called the pain/pleasure principle and is one of the primary driving forces behind all human behavior. Every decision we make is driven by these components. It is unmistakable and undeniable. Our brain has an internal scale that is constantly weighing the pain/pleasure outcome of our decision making. We are hard-wired to gain pleasure and avoid pain. A recent study published in the Journal of Consumer Psychology (Hardisty & Weber, 2020) essentially showed that we want to have pleasurable things as soon as possible and delay bad things as long as possible. Unfortunately, much of our activity occurs in the *strong desire to avoid pain.* This discussion leads us to the conclusion that one of the cores of all motivation is our brain's weighing the pain/pleasure outcome of a certain decision/activity. Depending on the situation, the brain does more to avoid pain than it does to gain pleasure. I examine the depth of simple questions such as why do women put on makeup in the morning, or not? Why do we exercise? Who, here, procrastinates? Everyone raises their hands, and then I get some specific examples. Why? Again, a variety of answers. I then continue with this statement: The reason you procrastinate is because the pleasure of not doing something (whatever it is they are putting off) is greater than the pain of doing it; plain and simple. What happens when two pains come up side by side (you've procrastinated so long that you now have to complete the painful activity)? If it is something like the RTC project, the pain of not doing it now wins (no grade, no tuition reimbursement, lose your certification, no pay raise, etc.), and you can no longer procrastinate. It now becomes more painful not to do the project. More than a decade ago, I saw a CAT scan of my heart, which already showed calcification in the arteries in and around it! It moved me. It made eating well and becoming aerobically fit a must. It was a real epiphany, and I made some major changes in my life. The pleasure of eating what I wanted no longer outweighed the pain of that CAT scan and what that could mean for my future and the future of my family.

## PAIN/PLEASURE IN PRACTICE

The following activities are meant to give you an insight into what you attach pleasure to and what you associate with pain.

Name three things you do to avoid pain.

1. .............................................................................................................

2. .............................................................................................................

3. .............................................................................................................

Name three things you do to gain pleasure.

1. .............................................................................................................

2. .............................................................................................................

3. .............................................................................................................

List three actions that you have been putting off that you need to take right now. Is it a phone call that needs to be made? Do you need to begin exercising? Do you need to make a doctor's appointment? Is there something you need to communicate to someone else? Do you need to lose weight or stop smoking? Have you been interested in some professional activity you just haven't taken the time to research and use?

1. .............................................................................................................

2. .............................................................................................................

3. .............................................................................................................

List the pain you've associated with these particular actions. Has it been too painful to make the call? Why? What pain have you associated with not eating in a more healthful manner (as an example)?

1. .............................................................................................................

2. .............................................................................................................

3. .............................................................................................................

List all the pleasure you've received by not doing this or these action(s) now.

1. ................................................................................

2. ................................................................................

3. ................................................................................

Write down the opposite effect of your nonaction. What will it cost you if you don't take the action; next week, next year, in ten years; financially, for your health, for your life's purposes, in terms of relationships? *Make it emotional! This is what takes something from being a "should" to being a "must." It is the process of getting leverage on yourself so you ACT!*

1. ................................................................................

2. ................................................................................

3. ................................................................................

Finally, list what you will gain if you take immediate action!

1. ................................................................................

2. ................................................................................

3. ................................................................................

You can advertise in your own mind to set up the pleasurable associations you desire instead of having someone else do it to you, which marketers and advertisers make a career of! The pain/pleasure principle is constantly at work in our lives. Teachers need to know how it works in their lives and be comfortable with the concept so they can recognize it in students. Not doing homework or doing homework is a pain/pleasure issue. Being excited about learning or school is a pain/pleasure issue. Remember, the key to using the pain/pleasure principle in your own life is to focus on the pain of not doing something and the subsequent cost to your life. What will it cost you if you don't take this action? Unfortunately, avoiding pain is the greater of these two forces, and focusing on what we'll lose or the consequences then becomes the more potent motivator.

I write about pain and pleasure because, personally, it has become a simple tool for me to do a gut check that reveals my motives, motivations, and levels of desire. My wife understands the pain/pleasure issue well, and we often say to each other "it's a pain/pleasure issue" whether it's regarding a choice to procrastinate yet again or drive forward and complete a task or goal. What I've learned to do is to recognize the cost of my inaction to my goals and quality of life. That drives and fuels me. What if I don't take this action? What will it cost me? I'm going to be asking you to do things throughout this book. Whether it is to be more physically active, manage your stress, set goals, create a personal mission statement, or create a morning routine that will ignite and drive you, make no mistake—your decision to partake or not is a pain/pleasure issue. Sizing up the cost of your action or inaction could determine the quality of your personal and professional life and have an unmistakable impact on the students you teach.

# HABIT #1

## LIVE THE PHYSICAL LIFE

FROM YOUR GENES TO YOUR EMOTIONS, YOUR BODY AND BRAIN ARE DYING TO EMBRACE THE PHYSICAL LIFE. YOU ARE BUILT TO MOVE. WHEN YOU DO, YOU'LL BE ON FIRE.

DR. JOHN RATEY

 **IN THIS CHAPTER YOU'LL READ ABOUT**

- The brain/body connection
- Your physiology's influence on your psychology
- The correlation between living a physical life and leading a successful one
- Physical activity and stress reduction
- Exercise hints and tips
- The benefits of creating a physical classroom

## A PARADIGM SHIFT

In his stunning book *Spark: The Revolutionary New Science of Exercise and the Brain*, Harvard associate clinical professor of Psychiatry, Dr. John Ratey (2008) describes exercise as "elevating Miracle-Gro throughout the brain." One significant study showed that aerobic exercise was as effective as antidepressants. Our understanding of the brain-body connection may indeed be the most exciting scientific advance of the 21st century. It is basic to the human experience, and your heightened awareness of it will increase your opportunity to lead a passionate, purpose-driven life. Your brain has a powerful influence on your body—your thoughts matter. Conversely, we now know that the body has a profound impact on your brain; they exist for each other's benefit or demise and are extensions of each other. The brain requires that the body move. As we age, we are also concerned about brain health. The most profound thing you can do to preserve optimal cognitive functioning might be to find your sneakers.

My gradual awakening to this relationship occurred in the early 2000s while preparing to teach a graduate course on brain-based teaching and learning. A keen interest became an intense professional curiosity and served to strengthen and support my own personal goals grounded in fitness, nutrition, and stress management. The brain/body relationship became the glue that bonded the three and made greater sense of them in a more holistic way. Similarly, exercise was taking on a whole new meaning for me personally. My sole purpose as a young man was to build muscle quickly. As I aged, my focus turned more toward aerobic conditioning to ensure my cardiovascular health. Now, understanding the role fitness plays in brain health, perspective, and outlook, I have even more to gain from a good sweat.

More so than any other component of a life well lived, the line of communication between the brain and body impacts each moment, thought, choice, and action. "We are what we think" in large part creates our destiny, impacts our state of mental and physical health, and should give us all great pause to take care to nourish our brains and bodies with uplifting thoughts. This leads to a continual "taking stock" of our belief systems to make sure we are creating positivity rather than negativity. Both have a profound effect on the body.

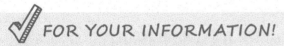 FOR YOUR INFORMATION!

**Your physiology can change your psychology.**

Your body can instantly change your brain and the way you feel. Movement creates momentum. Movement creates energy. Movement creates motivation. I know through research and experience that if I'm feeling bad, sad, stressed, angry, bored, and/or listless, my body is usually looking and feeling the same way. I also know that by simply changing my posture to standing tall, chin up and shoulders back, and by putting a smile on my face I can instantly change the way I feel. When we smile, we feel happy, but when we force ourselves to smile, we can feel happier. I've also learned that when I'm feeling a negative emotion, I'm usually sitting or lying. As soon as I stand and move to create a different level of energy, I immediately feel better. Sports teams don't sit quietly to prepare for a sporting event. They move, speak loudly, yell, cheer, high-five, and create synergy.

So can you. The problem is that most people don't take advantage of these simple techniques.

In what is one of the most viewed TED Talks ever, "Your Body Language May Shape Who You Are," Amy Cuddy (2012) shares research that indicates certain power poses that expand our physical selves (think Wonder Woman or raising your hands high in the air while standing with your feet shoulder width apart) actually raise testosterone levels while lowering cortisol levels. Conversely, powerless poses that make us smaller such as sitting with your legs crossed and arms folded actually lower testosterone levels and raise levels of cortisol. She highlights her talk with the following mantra:

*Our bodies change our minds,*

*Our minds change our behaviors,*

*Our behaviors change our outcomes.*

**Perfect.**

All this originates with the brain/body connection. Trying to create a well-balanced and influential life without a clear vision of this relationship is a bit like driving to a new destination without directions. You might arrive, but it will be later rather than sooner. Each morning I make a renewed commitment to powerful thought and purposeful physical activity, knowing that it will make or break my day based on the reality created by both my body and brain . . . together. I encourage you to do the same. You will become an even better teacher, role model, and influencer for your students.

# 🔍 REFLECTION

Take a moment to reflect on the brain/body connection in your own life. What are the thoughts that hold you back and create stress? What are the thoughts that push you forward and create feelings of flow and joy? How have you used your body to purposefully make yourself feel better?

Write your response here:

.............................................................................................................................................

.............................................................................................................................................

.............................................................................................................................................

.............................................................................................................................................

## EMBRACING THE PHYSICAL LIFE DOES MUCH MORE THAN RAISE YOUR LEVEL OF FITNESS

I recently delivered a keynote to a group of physical education professionals. The focus of the talk was the significant nature of a physical educator's influence that had little to do with fitness and health. Instead, it has everything to do with the surprising benefits of embracing the physical life for reasons that underscore the importance of moving or being active for a successful life. I'd like to share a short excerpt here.

I am here today to talk with you about the soul of physical activity, and that is emotion. All of us . . . are . . . our . . . emotions. Emotions are the driving force behind all our lives. Rarely do we do anything without trying to change the way we feel. Rarely does anything happen to us without it changing the way we feel. And where there is motion and physical activity, there is emotion, and that is what has, in large part, pushed my life forward. When we talk about emotion, when we think about emotion, and as I look back over my life, there have been two or three instances, pivotal moments in time, where my life changed dramatically in new, unimaginable ways. And I'm not being overly dramatic. As I look back with the benefit of hindsight, hopefully some wisdom, and definitely age, each one of those instances was proceeded by a physical challenge and a physical success; my definition of success. It's been amazing to go back and witness.

I was not a good student. In fact, I barely graduated from high school. This best-selling author got two Ds and two Fs his senior year in English and had to pass photography just to have enough credits to graduate. By the skin of my teeth, I passed English, graduated, and went on to college as a miserable business major. I was bad at that, too. During my first two years, in college my lowest GPA was a 1.57. My highest semester was a 2.2. You have to actually work to get grades like that.

But while all this bad was happening academically, something really wonderful was happening in another part of my life. The earth was moving beneath me. This kid, who graduated from high school at about 5'8" and 140 lbs., found a weight room. My life changed forever. For the first time in my life, I had a sense of direction. For the first time in my life, I had a dedication I had never known before. For the first time in my life, I had a discipline I'd never known before. And for the first time in my life, I had a desire I had never known. I had a newfound confidence. I liked the way I looked, I liked the way I felt, I held myself differently, I walked differently, felt better, and had a new motivation that was driving my life forward. In fact, I entered my first and only two bodybuilding competitions at ages 19 and 20. Though I was a very average competitor, what I was gaining from this experience was amazing. I was learning how to manipulate my body through weight training and nutrition. Current research reports that I was most likely getting smarter as weight training is showing some of the same benefits as aerobic activity with regard to cognition. I now had momentum in my life that was very physical. I was pushing hard, pushing forward, becoming more disciplined and motivated in all areas of my life, and less than four months after my final bodybuilding competition, at the height of my newfound dedication, my newfound discipline, and my newfound motivation, the unthinkable happened . . . I became a music major.

You might be saying "so"? The thing is, I was almost twenty-one years of age and had never played or read a note of music. During this period of time, I transferred to a new university. After another poor, and what felt like wasted, first semester, I had another problem. I couldn't get into my upper-level business courses because I hadn't passed the required computer course. At my previous institution I either got Ds or Fs, so those courses didn't transfer. Back then, a computer course meant taking COBOL or Fortran. What? Fortunately for me, taking a computer course had recently turned into personal computing with IBM computers and floppy disks bigger than my head. I was actually able to handle that, but it also meant that I had a spring semester where the only course I could take was that single computer course. Instead of looking for a job, I opened up the course catalog and searched. I actually thought, "You know what? I like music more than most people," so I signed up for a 20th-century music course because I thought it was going to be about the Beatles, Led Zeppelin, and the Rolling Stones. Hmm . . . turns out it was about Stravinsky, Copland, and Rimsky-Korsakov, but to my surprise, I liked it. I then decided to register for an Introduction to Music course, and within about a month, I fell in love.

I marched into the music department chair's office and told her that I wanted to be a music major, and she asked what I played, and I said "nothing," of course. Hiding her shock and amusement, she eventually relented, and I had to choose an instrument. This is still embarrassing to admit, but I liked the way the saxophone sounded and also liked the way it looked on Rob Lowe in *St. Elmo's Fire*. I was hooked. Over the next two years, I earned a BA in music and never got below a 3.5 GPA. All this success I was now having I could trace right back to the momentum that was created from my physical life—the dedication, discipline, desire, and motivation. I was still in the gym five days a week and began running as well.

After a year of working and studying the saxophone privately, I made the single best decision of my life, although I didn't know it at the time. I left my family, my close-knit group of friends, and my comfort zone—because that is where the juice of life is lived. I love the quote "To get to the fruit of the tree you have to go out on a limb." So, at age twenty-three, I moved 2,000 miles away from Pennsylvania to Colorado. I earned a master's degree in music education and a teaching certificate at the University of Northern Colorado. Colorado was where my teaching career began, where I met my wife, and where my twins were born. It was the best nine years of my life. All of it—this newfound success and happiness—I credit to the momentum created by my physical life.

There are many more instances where my physical journey profoundly influenced my life's success. In my view, the greatest of these was a decision to participate in the Broad Street Run, a ten-mile road race down Broad Street in the great city of Philadelphia. This journey, from never having run more than four miles to preparing for a ten-miler over an eleven-week period, changed me. Once again, the dedication, drive, discipline, and desire that was required of me supercharged my daily living. On race day, surrounded by 25,000 other runners, I experienced a tenth and final mile that was by far my fastest. As I sprinted across the finish line in front of thousands of cheering people, at forty-four years of age, I felt like I could do anything I set my mind to. That is power. If I could take on this physical challenge and dominate it, I could do anything. My nervous system was becoming hardwired to believe that if I could take on a physical challenge and experience success that it would transform the rest of my life—my emotional life, my intellectual life, my professional life, my academic life, and my social life. I was now beginning to use that physical momentum to purposefully power forward.

Armed with that level of energy and motivation, less than eight months after the Broad Street Run, I had written my first book—*The Kinesthetic Classroom: Teaching and Learning Through Movement*. It became a best seller and was a game changer for me personally. Not only was it professionally significant and satisfying, but also conferences that weren't even letting me present were asking me to keynote. I was traveling the United States doing professional development, and just a few short years later, I was traveling all over the world. Not only did my life change dramatically once again, but I was also living the life of my dreams. I traveled to places I would have never visited and experienced amazing things in places like Johannesburg, Tokyo, Kuala Lumpur, Manila, and Barcelona. It was a new level of living, a new level of joy, and one that could all be traced back to my physical life—the physical challenge and the physical success.

## AMBER'S BROAD STREET STORY

**At one time, the race website contained personal narratives of the "Broad Street" experience. One in particular, the story of Amber, stood out. I was so moved that I immediately contacted her, and with her permission, would like to share her race story with you:**

*I was a smoker in high school and college. When one of my dearest friends was diagnosed with breast cancer, I threw the cigarettes away and tried frantically to think about what I could do to help her. I decided to run the Race for the Cure, another great event to fight cancer, in 2001. Having never run a step in my life, I trained hard. I was sore, coughing, and miserable for months. But I did it. I raised 500 dollars to fight breast cancer that year and got hooked on running.*

*A few years later I stood at the top of Broad Street in a sea of people, feeling very alone and scared. My heart felt like it was in my mouth as I crossed the start line. I remember passing the "Abominable Slow-Men" and laughing so hard I almost cried. I also saw a man running the race, juggling. I thought about my friend Maria, and how she inspired me. She just had her five-year cancer-free "birthday."*

*The theme from Rocky carried me into the Navy Yard. I was a back-of-the-pack finisher, arms held high, as if I was the first one to cross that line. I was barely able to walk down steps for two days, but strangely enough, Broad Street 2007, here I come again!*

*To those who think they cannot do this, you are wrong! Find your strength, what matters to you, and do it. I will be there, somewhere in the ten-minute mile pack, waiting with you at the top of Broad Street, and crossing with you at the Navy Yard.*

Amber's "Broad Street" run turned out to be just another stepping-stone in her journey. She went on to run the 2007 Philadelphia Marathon. For those of you who don't know, that's 26.2 miles. As for her friend Maria, she remains cancer-free, and despite doctors telling her she would never be able to have children, her bundle of joy is three years old.

Amber's act of love inspired her to change her life through fitness. Bruce Barton perfectly describes her unselfishness:

> Nothing splendid has ever been achieved except by those who dared believe that something inside them was superior to circumstance

If you could harness the power that the physical life has to offer to change your existence radically, would you take advantage? Why would you not?

> I always loved running . . . it was something you could do by yourself, and under your own power. You could go in any direction, fast or slow as you wanted, fighting the wind if you felt like it, seeking out new sights just on the strength of your feet and the courage of your lungs.

> Jesse Owens

# REFLECTION

Take a moment to reflect on physical activity in your life. Has there been a time when the momentum from moving pushed your life forward with vigor? Created a new success? If not to date, how might physical activity support your endeavors?

Write your response here:

...........................................................................................................................

...........................................................................................................................

...........................................................................................................................

...........................................................................................................................

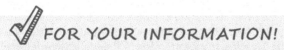 FOR YOUR INFORMATION!

Research on physical activity indicates the following:

- Just a small amount of movement increases dopamine and norepinephrine—neurotransmitters that aid attention and focus (Ratey, 2008).
- Exercise in midlife is connected to better brain health in late life (Palta et al., 2021).
- Physical exercise may do more to prevent cardiovascular disease than previously known (Ramakrishnan et al., 2021).
- Just eleven minutes of physical activity a day can boost your life expectancy (Ekelund et al., 2020) and counter the effects of sitting.
- Physical activity has been shown to increase neurogenesis or the creation of new brain cells (Ratey, 2008).
- Physical activity lessens the symptoms of stress, anxiety, depression, ADHD, addiction, hormonal changes, and dementia (Ratey, 2008).
- Physical exercise improves mood and boosts happiness (Fisher, 2020).

*(Continued)*

(Continued)

Aerobic exercise—such as walking, jogging, swimming, and cycling—lowers blood sugar and insulin levels, blood pressure, reduces stress, and raises good cholesterol. Physically active people also enjoy better bone, lung, and heart health and have an easier time managing their weight. But these are all side effects. The true beneficiary of aerobic fitness is your brain. Dr. Ratey (2008) says that exercising is like taking a little bit of Ritalin and a little bit of Prozac without the side effects. When the body moves, the brain naturally balances its neurochemicals. That is why it feels so good when you finish a walk, bike ride, or swim, especially after feeling high amounts of stress. All of us experience periodic stress. Thankfully, our bodies are well-equipped for the challenge. Unfortunately, chronic stress has become characteristic of modern life, and that is problematic. The good news is that any aerobic activity is an effective stress manager. How could it not be? Swimming, running, cycling, or hiking demand our focus and attention. It epitomizes living in the moment, where stressful thoughts are not allowed. On a biological level, exercise puts your body in a stressful situation, and in short doses, is not only healthful but necessary. I look forward to my workouts in part because I know I will experience active stress relief. You could equate exercising with receiving a low-dose vaccination. Exercising in response to stress is a simple and effective way to raise your body's ability to deal with the pressures of everyday life. As with meditation or deep breathing, exercise calms the body, making it possible to manage greater levels of turbulence.

## HIGH-PERFORMANCE ACTION!

**Try this simple experiment:**

The next time you feel overwhelmed by stress, hit the road, jump in the pool, or get on your bike, and don't stop for thirty minutes. When you've finished your workout, notice what has happened to your stress levels. They should have lessened or completely vanished. It is real, it is biological, and it can always be counted upon.

I entered my fifth decade in 2015, and it has not been without some significant physical challenges. In the past five years, I've experienced spine surgery (a microdiscectomy and laminectomy), a significant fall from my mountain bike (I had to be carried to the car on the way to the emergency room), the removal of two lipomas, and Covid-19. While these challenges set me back for unusually long amounts of time, I never strayed from moving every day that I was able. Physical activity is what rescued me from every setback. As you age, the less you tend to move and the more stiff and sore you become. I do not dare tempt a life without being physical. There is just too much at stake.

Are you aware of *anything* else available to us that can so positively impact our health, productivity, life expectancy, brain health, and motivation? *Can you make any other conclusion than regular physical activity is a miracle of life?* Yet, to paraphrase neurokinesthesiologist, Jean Moize, "we live in a culture of sitness versus fitness" and Dr. John Ratey, "we are literally shriveling our brains because of it."

### How will you begin to move?

# REFLECTION

In a perfect world with fewer time commitments and fewer ailments, aches, pains, and health challenges, what exercise(s) would you choose to perform on a daily basis? For how long? What pleasure do you gain by not exercising regularly? What pain do you experience when you do exercise regularly? What will it cost you and your loved ones if you remain sedentary?

Write your response here:

..............................................................................................................................

..............................................................................................................................

..............................................................................................................................

..............................................................................................................................

## EXERCISE IS LIFE'S FIRST ANSWER TO THIS ESSENTIAL QUESTION: HOW DO I CREATE A LIFE WORTH LIVING?

Edward Stanley says it this way:

> *Those who think they have no time for bodily exercise will sooner or later have to find time for illness.*

Far too many people test his theory. All you aspire to be is jeopardized through an inactive lifestyle. Exercise provides a better brain, body, and perspective, which make you more effective. It is simplistic at its core, yet remains elusive for many.

Jack LaLanne remains one of my personal inspirations. For more than eight decades he dedicated himself to a life of fitness. I would like to share a few of what have become affectionately known as LaLanneisms:

—Your waistline is your lifeline

—Exercise is king, nutrition is queen, put them together and you've got a kingdom

—People don't die of old age, they die of inactivity

—Do—don't stew

At age forty, Jack swam the length of the Golden Gate Bridge underwater with 140 pounds of equipment, including two air tanks. At age sixty, he swam from Alcatraz Island to Fisherman's Wharf while handcuffed, shackled, and towing thirteen boats containing seventy-six people. And, at eighty, he received the State of California's Governor's Council on Physical Fitness Lifetime Achievement Award. Right up until his death at age ninety-six, he lived by this motto: "I can't die, it will ruin my image."

It is never too late.

> *It's an act of love to take care of your body.*
>
> Louise Hay

I am often asked a prefaced question: If I have thirty minutes, several days a week, to dedicate to exercise, what activity would provide the most benefit? For me, the answer is simple: something aerobic. There are so many wonderful ways to invigorate yourself through exercise, but walking, swimming, running, cycling, and so on provide the most quality return on your investment of time. If you are making a new decision to become regularly physically active or to reignite your past exercise practice, I suggest you heed the words of Thomas Jefferson:

*Of all exercises walking is the best.*

*Thomas Jefferson*

## SIMPLY . . . WALK

Walking is a near-perfect form of exercise. It allows for flexibility of schedule and location. It builds your aerobic capacity and easily allows for increasing intensity by traveling longer distances or moving more quickly. I know of a man who, in his fifties, was determined to walk a half-hour each day. He accomplished that goal and eventually walked a marathon! This practice can also lead to other activities, like slow jogging. If you can slowly jog around the track once, it can lead to slowly jogging around the track twice. By adding one lap every two weeks you'll be ready for your first 5k run in about three months! What a tremendous accomplishment! Your first day of walking is no different from your tenth year of running; you must continually challenge yourself to make progress.

## WHERE ARE YOUR SNEAKERS?

*A limit on what you will do puts a limit on what you can do.*

*Dexter Yager*

I write this first chapter hoping to move and push you, motivate and excite you, challenge and ignite you through stories, research, and even your own reflections so you are more equipped to push through self-imposed limitations and roadblocks. By engaging in the physical life, you'll renew yourself and be better for your students each and every day. Here is a simple truth about fitness: No matter your shape, size, or condition, you can change your life today through exercise. Its immediate benefits will have your body singing with joy!

To get you started I offer you the following:

 SIMPLE HINTS AND TIPS

1. Exercising must be scheduled. No appointment is more important.

2. Proper workout attire is a must. For example, if you are a novice walker/runner, being properly fitted for shoes is critical for both comfort and safety.

3. Balance your fitness plan. Yoga is a great example of incorporating flexibility, strength, and endurance all at once!

4. Vary your workouts, and change scenery often. It will help you stay motivated and fresh.

5. Make sure to drink plenty of water—there is a direct correlation between peak athletic performance and hydration.

6. You must continue to challenge yourself. The body plateaus quickly.

7. Preworkout warm-ups and post-workout stretching go a long way in preventing injury.

8. Fitness and supportive nutrition go hand in hand.

9. People who listen to music while they exercise are more likely to exercise and less likely to quit.

10. A workout partner can make a big difference.

Apocrypha said, "A faithful friend is the medicine of life." Truer words have not been spoken. Through the years, I have had the great pleasure of exercising with many different friends, which brings certain gifts to the table. Being responsible to someone else is naturally motivating and helps ensure safety during a workout. The achievement of goals, and the setting of new ones, renders greater satisfaction when shared. Most importantly, a workout partner can provide that gentle nudge when needed. I have nothing but sincere gratitude to all those individuals who have supported, pushed, and encouraged me. We've shared mostly laughter but also a few tears; mostly progress but also a few setbacks; but most importantly, we've shared shoulders to lean on when the last mile seemed impossible.

*The long road becomes shorter when shared with a friend.*

## VARY THE ENVIRONMENT

I once heard a personal trainer tell a client that "balance was the key to fitness." That was a great lesson for me. Since that day, nature has become a true inspiration. I look forward to finding new ways to experience the outdoors and be true to my fitness goals. As important as it is to balance your fitness needs between muscular strength, endurance, and flexibility, it is equally important to vary workout venues. Every autumn, I kayak in Blue Mountain Lake, which is nestled in the Adirondack Mountains of New York. My mind cannot dream of a more beautiful setting. Blue skies, brilliantly colored trees, and crisp air provide a scene that is at once both serene and motivating. I give great thanks that I can be physically active and enjoy such beauty at the same time. I call it "peaceful exertion." I've learned to appreciate that exercise need not be confined to a fitness center but can be experienced on trails, in lakes, and on mountaintops.

# REFLECTION

It is now time to use your greatest of personal powers—to make a decision and to act. You might be a regular exerciser, someone who used to exercise more frequently, or someone who has never exercised at all. It doesn't matter! All of us can choose to act now to become more physically active to be better at life and better for our students—to become a Peak Performing Teacher. What are you committed to doing today? If not today, then tomorrow by the latest? What form of physical activity/exercise will you commit to? Can you commit to daily exercise even if it is only fifteen minutes in duration? What time of day? How much time will you spend performing the exercise? Will you ask a friend to join you? What equipment will you need? Will you make use of music? Planning to exercise is one thing, but scheduling it makes it real! Please be detailed in your response.

Write your response here:

........................................................................................................................

........................................................................................................................

........................................................................................................................

## THE BENEFITS DON'T STOP AT SCHOOL (A WORD ABOUT THE PHYSICAL CLASSROOM)

When you make the decision to enjoy the physical life, it will have an immediate impact on your students. Not only will you have more energy, stamina, and inspiration, but you'll also serve as a role model for a generation of children who have been plagued by fast food, obesity, lack of fitness and physical activity, and ever-increasing screen time. There is almost no more powerful yet subtle role in which you'll serve your students. If you don't exercise for yourself, do it for them. If your life is currently not as physical as it could be, think about your students. Would you want them to experience the physical life? Could it benefit them socially, emotionally, and academically? In fact, you might consider immersing them in a physical classroom.

*Learning doesn't happen from the neck up, it happens from the feet up.*

Creating a physical or kinesthetic classroom has many educational benefits. It represents the brain/body connection in real time. A large part of my professional career has been spent educating teachers and administrators about the benefits of creating a kinesthetic classroom. Aside from an increase in the joy of learning, physical activity in the learning ecosystem also promotes the following:

- Differentiation
- Motivation
- Reduced sitting time
- Stress reduction
- Attention
- Retention
- Executive function development
- Management of learning states

- Sensory engagement
- Implicit learning
- Episodic memory
- Classroom management through the meeting of basic human needs

In our 2010 book, *The Kinesthetic Classroom: Teaching and Learning Through Movement*, Traci Lengel and I proposed a six-level framework for using physical activity to enhance the teaching and learning process. The framework includes the following:

1. Preparing the brain to learn, which promotes activities that specifically ready the brain for learning

2. Providing brain breaks, which gives students a short break from content to refocus, raise alertness, and re-energize

3. Supporting exercise and fitness through one-to-five-minute intense bouts of heartrate raising physical activities to support physical fitness and alertness

4. Creating class cohesion to build community, collaboration, cooperation, and an emotionally engaging classroom climate

5. Reviewing content through unique and engaging physical activities that involve all learners

6. Teaching content to engage the brain through more implicit learning opportunities by taking advantage of the way the brain learns naturally through emotion and movement

What we often miss out on in classroom instruction is creating the best learner possible to deal with large amounts of content. While there are many factors beyond your control, you can create better learners instantly through the use of movement in the teaching and learning process. Creating a classroom based in physical activity will also serve as a critical example to your students of the power of movement and the fact that it does impact every area of their lives—that your physical life is critical to your academic life; that your physical life is critical to your emotional life; that your physical life is critical to a successful life. The younger students learn this, the better the chance that it can impact them for a lifetime. The more physically active you are in your own life, the more likely it is you'll bring a physicality to your teaching. The brain/body connection is always in play in every classroom no matter the age of the student. The more we know about it, the more we can take advantage of it in our teaching.

# REFLECTION

How can you be more of a role model for your students regarding the physical life? What can you do to create a more physical classroom?

Write your response here:

..................................................................................................................................

..................................................................................................................................

..................................................................................................................................

..................................................................................................................................

# HABIT #2

············································

## CHANGE YOUR MIND

# NOTHING IS GOOD OR BAD. IT IS THINKING THAT MAKES IT SO.

## WILLIAM SHAKESPEARE

 ## IN THIS CHAPTER YOU'LL READ ABOUT

- The role of fear in stress
- The impact of perspective on stress reduction
- Challenging negative thoughts and reframing them for better outcomes
- The power of breath, mindfulness, and meditation
- Humor and the brain/body connection
- Some brief thoughts on stress in the classroom

If you look closely enough there are gifts in all life events. In his book *Illusions: The Adventures of a Reluctant Messiah*, Richard Bach writes:

> There is no such thing as a problem without a gift for you in its hands. You seek problems because you need their gifts.

Stress is our body's natural response to perceived events, protecting and feeding us in a time of need. Stress is perfectly normal, natural, and healthy. But the stress response can be overdone; the accelerator pressed for too long, the brain sensing injury instead of recovery.

> Is everything as urgent as your stress would imply?
>
> Carrie Latet

The body will act to protect its interests, and by doing so, turn on itself with damaging effects. Sleep becomes a privilege, blood pressure rises, and the heart races more than it jogs. It takes an expensive toll physically, mentally, and most of all, emotionally.

> Give your stress wings and let it fly away.
>
> Carin Hartness

Perceived threats are ever-present, and your reactions to them are critical to your well-being. Our perceptions are based on our belief systems. These core beliefs cause us to love some things and fear others. This brings to light a prophetic, yet simple truth:

## Underneath most stress lies quietly a fear.

There was a point in my teaching career where my stress became unbearable. It wasn't the normal, day-to-day stressors that were concerning, it was a personal attack from a parent that had me reeling. His attack was unwarranted, and I had the full support of my supervisor, but that didn't matter. My skin had not grown thick enough at this point in my career. I had never dealt with anything like it before. This particular parent was not happy with the job I was doing. What I didn't know then, but know now, is that I was letting the situation control me instead of using my perspective to control it. Fortunately, I've gotten to the point that I'm truly grateful for the experience. That parent was an angel in disguise. Because of this situation, I learned how to manage my stress more effectively. I turned to meditation and learned how to recognize the fear underlying my stress. What was I afraid of? Why was it causing me stress? At its core I was afraid of not having this person's approval for the work I was doing. I wasn't scared of losing my job, but I was frightened that someone didn't think highly of me. It might sound silly, but it was very real and honest for me. If I had been able to identify that fear I might have been able to deal with it more effectively. Coming to terms with fear is a key to managing stress. I now subscribe to a simple two-step process for beating the stress that mostly exists "between our ears."

Step 1

Identify the fear that is causing your stress. People try to deal with the symptoms of stress rather than with the fear that causes it in the first place.

Step 2

Answer the following three questions:

1) Is the fear realistic? This helps create perspective.

2) What is the worst possible thing that could happen? This also helps create perspective.

3) How can I move past this fear? This creates action.

Often, the answers to these questions will help relieve your stress or cause you to act in chasing it away.

*Comfort your fears, list them, get to know them, and only then will you be able to put them aside and move ahead.*

*Jerry Gillies*

Fear can serve as a great teacher as long as its shackles do not imprison. Welcome your challenges with an open mind and heart; overcoming them makes the next joy sweeter.

*Only when we are no longer afraid do we begin to live.*

*Dorothy Thompson*

As I described, I feared not having this particular parent's approval. Was this fear realistic? In part, yes. In part, no. While he was disappointed in my performance, he never indicated he didn't like me or that he had anything against me personally. I was not able to differentiate the two. What was the worst thing that could possibly happen? I wasn't going to lose my job, so not too much. The worst possible thing that could have happened was to have a very frank conversation with this parent about his concerns and how we should move forward. How could I have moved past this fear? By taking a step back and looking at the reality of the situation and realizing that it wasn't nearly as bad as I was making it out to be—my choice; my perspective; my stress. I had the option to change my mind. I just didn't even realize that I had a choice!

In the spring of the same school year, I took the concert, jazz, and marching bands to Virginia for a weekend of intense competition—and fun. I've never worked harder to prepare students for performance. During the morning of the second day, all three bands competed. The entire year's preparation culminated on this one day. I was quietly very stressed but was very proud of the effort of these young musicians. The rest of the day was spent in an amusement park where the kids could finally let loose, have fun, and not have me breathing down their necks. Me? Not so much. I had so much stress thinking about the evening awards ceremony and was so tired from everything that lead to this moment, I could barely move. I did not yet have the ability to change my perspective and was completely letting events control me. My body finally shut down, and I fell asleep at a table right in the middle of the bustling amusement park. As it turns out, we could not have performed much better. Every band rated in the highest category, and we won numerous individual and group awards. The relief was overtaking my brain and body. While this should not have been what relieved my year of stress, it certainly helped.

Two years later, I received a letter of thanks from this very parent for the wonderful experience his son had during our time together. It was an apology without saying I'm sorry but one that was certainly good enough for me. In turn, I should have written a thank you note to this "angel."

# REFLECTION

Take a moment to reflect on a school-related stressor. Can you identify a fear that is causing or has caused this particular stress? Is the fear realistic? What is the worst thing that could possibly happen? Is it possible to move past the fear and relieve the stress? What steps would you need to take?

Write your response here:

................................................................................................................................

................................................................................................................................

................................................................................................................................

................................................................................................................................

## CHALLENGE YOUR THINKING

Identifying the way experiences or events are viewed in order to challenge and change thought patterns would have been helpful to me in overcoming this perception-induced stress. Research suggests that cognitive reframing, or changing the way we perceive a stressful situation, can help alleviate the stress. It becomes a path to "changing your mind." Along with identifying my fear and exactly what was causing my stress, it would have been useful to have analyzed my initial adverse thought processes as follows:

"I can't believe he thinks I'm doing a terrible job."

"I am doing a terrible job."

"Do others think I'm doing a terrible job?"

If I had done that it would have been easier to identify contradictory evidence to my initial negative thinking, such as follows:

"My supervisor completely supports me."

"No other parent has complained about the work I'm doing."

"The majority of parents think I'm doing a wonderful job."

"I think I'm doing a good job and don't need the approval of others."

"Can I learn anything from his comments to improve?"

The above statements and question are more reasonable and rational. This sort of reasoning would have helped to control my perception and corresponding stress.

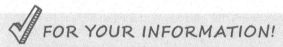

## FOR YOUR INFORMATION!

- Cognitive restructuring has been used successfully to treat a wide variety of conditions, including depression, posttraumatic stress disorder (PTSD), addictions, anxiety, social phobias, relationship issues, and stress.

# REFLECTION

In the example you previously cited, what were your initial thoughts that caused the stress response? What more realistic thoughts might you have used instead to transition the experience to a more positive one?

Write your response here:

.................................................................................................................................

.................................................................................................................................

.................................................................................................................................

.................................................................................................................................

*we can't solve problems by using the same kind of thinking we used when we created them.*

*Albert Einstein*

## SAME STORY, NEW MORAL

To make a point about how quickly our brains and bodies go into action when a threat is perceived, I often tell this story:

It was the Saturday after Thanksgiving in 2007, and my young family was tired, irritable, and most of all, hungry. Anybody who has changed a residence understands the difficulty in finding cookware, or food, on the day of the big move. Having drawn the short straw to go find a suitable dinner, I made off to the store, armed with a list. I entered the self-checkout line and successfully scanned seven bags of food. I pleasantly envisioned my family's first dinner together in our new home. Noticing the line behind me growing considerably, I quickly slid a credit card through the card reader. "Please try again," it read. I tried again; *declined*. The stress alarm began ringing in full force.

The empathy always grows in the room as I continue my story . . .

My body warmed, and my pulse began racing. I was in fight or flight. Staring customers and a hungry family dominated my thoughts. "What do I do with all these groceries?" I pondered. I handed my card to the self-checkout clerk. It didn't work for her either. I had no cell phone and no cash with me. The reality of the situation was beginning to take hold. No matter what the people behind me thought, and no matter how much scorn I faced at home, I would have to leave with no food. And I did just that. I knew I had paid my bill on time, and there was plenty of credit left on my account. Then it dawned on me what had happened. This particular card carried with it so much security that every so often the bank wanted to make sure it was really me who was using it! "Couldn't you have checked that another time?" I asked of the agent on the other end of the line. "Possibly when I was not standing in the grocery store self-checkout with seven bags of groceries and fourteen people staring at me?" It was pointless, and it didn't matter. Now cleared with full security, I went back to the store to pick up what I had left.

There was one particular time that upon finishing this story, a hand rose slowly from the audience. A gentleman with an uncomfortable grin on his face had a question, or comment—I was not sure which. "Yes?" I asked. "I had my identity stolen," exclaimed the man who would single-handedly change the point of this story.

You see where this is going . . .

"I love the fact that my bank makes sure that I am the only one who is using my credit card. It's not a bother. In fact, it's a relief." The room went silent. All eyes were upon me waiting to hear my reaction. Straight from my brain to my mouth came the most intellectual response I could muster, "Oh." From that point on the lecture changed; new moral noted:

### One person's stress is another person's joy.

Stress is nothing more than our response to any given moment in time. Change your mind, change your life! We always have multiple perceptual responses from which to choose. Choose well.

*The tragic or the humorous is a matter of perspective.*

*Arnold Brisser*

Peaceful Loving Grateful Caring Understanding Happy Appreciative Joyful Gleeful Glad Jolly Pleased Jubilant Playful Light Tender Pleasant Affectionate Enthusiastic Blissful Elated Lively Thrilled Cheerful Mirthful Ecstatic Overjoyed Content Delighted Humorous Tickled Festive Blessed Sparkling Upbeat Giving Friendly Serene Kind Mindful Generous Jubilant Thoughtful Gentle Blessed Upbeat Elated Lively Gratified Harmonious

## FIFTY STATES OF MIND WHERE STRESS CANNOT EXIST

### LESSON ON A WALK

I have the great fortune of working for someone who is my professional role model. Diana Ramsey is unquestionably the spiritual leader of our company. As president, she helped to grow the Regional Training Center by aspiring to change classrooms, one teacher at a time. Her vision and wisdom over the past three decades have taken RTC from what was literally a humble beginning in the basement of her home to a multimillion-dollar educational consulting firm. She regularly inspires me to stay focused on what is most important in life. Long before I was tuned into the concept of mindfulness, I particularly remember one walk we took together. During our conversation, she noticed my stress levels were a bit high due to my schedule in the coming weeks. As we walked, she began pointing out subtle signs of animals, highlighting different types of trees, and generally impressing me with her grasp of natural life.

More importantly, I was also receiving a crucial life lesson. She finished with this thought:

You cannot live mindfully, and at the same time, be upset about what is staring down at you—they are incompatible.

> The more closely we pay attention to the moment, the further away our troubles sail.

From that day forward, I made a conscious effort to be present in the moment. It affords me two rewards—basking in the glow of life and reducing unnecessary stress.

*Life is a succession of moments. To live each one is to succeed.*

*Corita Kent*

By definition, mindfulness is the fact or condition of being present;

paying attention in a particular way:

on purpose, in the present moment and nonjudgmentally;

the repetitive act of directing one's attention to only one thing in this one moment.

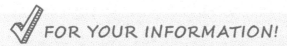 FOR YOUR INFORMATION!

- Research on mindfulness indicates that it increases working memory capacity, relieves depressive symptoms, reduces stress, increases focus, and creates more cognitive flexibility (Davis & Hayes, 2012).

## HIGH-PERFORMANCE ACTION!

We miss much of the juice of life because we focus on distant thoughts. You cannot be stressed and be present. Try this exercise: Go outside for a walk, and notice everything you've been missing: the color of leaves, the smell of flowers, the sounds of birds, the dampness of the air. Force yourself to be mindful of your surroundings and also of your body's reaction to them. Invest in conversation this way. Your partner will be grateful. Invest in eating this way. Your palette will be grateful. In these moments you will find peace. Mindfulness is generally thought of as a time when we need to be quiet and meditative. But when I think about mindfulness, it is about being present instead of going through life barely noticing because we are focused on something that has already happened or on something that might happen. Mindfulness in the form of being present and paying attention is a great gift that brings peace.

## JUST BREATHE

When faced with a stressful situation, the first thing to leave us is often that which heals us: breath. I prove this to my students by having them stand and look intently at me. To the audience I identify myself as "A." I then instruct them to hold their bodies and heads still but shift their "eyes only" to another point across the room to which I assign the letter "B." When I say "A," they look at me. When I say "B," they are once again to only shift their eyes to the second spot. I start slowly A . . . B, A . . . B, then I begin to speed it up to the point that it is almost impossible to keep up with me. Suddenly I stop and ask, "What did you just stop doing?" Eventually someone gets the correct answer, but most don't even realize that they stopped breathing. I purposefully put them in a stressful situation to the point where either their breathing got very shallow, or they are holding their breath altogether. Yet, breathing is your body's first line of defense against stress. This activity is an adaptation of "Breath-less" from *Structured Exercises in Stress Management, Volume 1* (Tubesing & Tubesing, 1983).

The next time you notice your stress levels rise, *stop*, and breathe, of the long variety— in through the nose for four counts, hold for four counts, out through the mouth in four counts.

Do this several times, and your heart rate will slow. If it seems like common sense, it is, but we take the power of breath for granted.

You can also combine breathing with a bit of progressive muscle relaxation when sensing rising stress levels. Along with the breathing described above, simultaneously tense your shoulders, arms, and clenched fists during the inhale and hold while releasing the tension in your shoulders, arms, and clenched fists during the exhale. I would generally recommend doing this up to five times in a row to relieve stress.

> A healthy mind has an easy breath.
>
> Author Unknown

## THE POWERHOUSE

The power of breath, mindfulness, deep relaxation, and effective stress management beautifully converge during the practice of meditation. Greg Schweitzer, founder of Stress Reduction Resources, taught me how to meditate more than two decades ago. In fact, it is what pulled me out of my stress-induced funk related to the parent that challenged my teaching ability. One of the kindest men I have ever met, I credit Greg with changing my life. His technique of Effortless Meditation has afforded me years of peaceful practice; quiet, personal moments that seemingly transcend time. I often describe them as "magical." Daily meditation has the power to change your mind and your perspective without being consciously aware of the process. Inner peace is one of its profound gifts.

> Meditation is the tongue of the soul and the language of our spirit.
>
> Jeremy Taylor

An age-old practice, there is no one "right" way to meditate. It can be practiced anywhere. You can begin by employing these two simple strategies:

> *Sit comfortably in a chair with both feet firmly planted on the floor. Close your eyes for up to one minute. At the same time, relax and center yourself. Open your eyes for a moment, then close them again for another minute while again focusing on your relaxation and centering. Open your eyes again for just a moment. Finally, close your eyes and breathe deeply, slowly, and rhythmically, focusing and concentrating on your breath. Try this for five minutes and continue to extend your time as you become more practiced.*

*When you become comfortable with focused breathing, you might try adding a repeated word or phrase to your meditation. Known as a mantra, it is a fundamental aspect of transcendental meditation. I often suggest the use of the word "peace." To begin, use the same directions as noted above:*

*Sit comfortably in a chair with both feet firmly planted on the floor. Close your eyes for up to a minute. At the same time, relax and center yourself. Open your eyes for a moment, then close them again for another minute while again focusing on your relaxation and centering. Open your eyes again for just a moment. Finally, close your eyes and breathe deeply, slowly, and rhythmically, focusing and concentrating on your breath. Silently add the word "peace" in a repetitive manner, repeating this word over and over again. When your mind wanders gently bring your focus back to the repetition of "peace." Try this for five minutes. Extend your time as you become more practiced. Continue for up to twenty minutes.*

Greg taught me that meditation is not unlike the ocean. The waves on top of the ocean are like the thoughts that are always near the front of our mind. As we do a deep dive into a single meditation practice, our mind goes below the surface to where the ocean is calm and thoughts are not as disruptive. As our thoughts return, and they will, our brain returns to the top of the ocean where the waves and activity are much greater and more turbulent. As we return the focus to the mantra, in the case above to the repeated use of the word "peace," the calm recovers as we dive below the surface once again. It is not unusual, especially in the beginning, to fall asleep. Don't be surprised if your head droops at times or if you need to take a big breath every so often. Breathing slows dramatically during the meditative process. I still can recall how I felt after my first full session of meditation on my own. I could barely pick up the pen I needed to fill out a questionnaire. My writing slowed to a snail's pace, and the feeling of peace and relaxation overwhelmed me. I recommend that you start with five minutes and build in five-minute increments until you've reached twenty minutes in total. On a very good day, I will meditate twice.

Meditation is mind calming and body relaxing, which induces a deep state of rest where heart and breath rate decrease significantly. In the most stressful of times, it can be leaned on like an old friend. In all its simplicity, meditation has proven itself time and again to change minds; bringing an inner glow and vitality that is rarely seen.

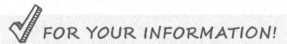 FOR YOUR INFORMATION!

- Research on meditation indicates that it reduces stress and other stress-related conditions such as posttraumatic stress disorder, lessens both anxiety and depression, can lead to a more positive outlook on life, raises self-awareness and helps individuals to better recognize destructive thought patterns, lengthens attention span, can reduce age-related memory loss, may help fight addictions, improves sleep, and decreases blood pressure (Thorpe & Link, 2020).

- If you are interested in Greg's work, visit www.StressReductionResources. com. Classes are provided in-person and online using live video conferencing.

Research is being conducted on meditation and its benefits for the brain such as preserving the aging brain by adding more gray matter volume. Meditation also seems to increase the volume of the hippocampus, a brain region critical to learning and memory, and to decrease brain cell volume in the amygdala, a region responsible for fear, anxiety, and stress (Walton, 2015).

The greatest gift that meditation can bring to your life is a change in perspective. How you actually view others and events has the possibility of changing. Where short-term stress management activities such as focused breathing or exercise can bring momentary relief, meditation can bring a long-term change in how we view the world. In my view, it is the powerhouse of stress relief.

## A QUICK REVISIT TO THE BRAIN/BODY CONNECTION

In Chapter 1, I introduced you to the brain/body connection. The recognition of the relationship between the brain and body is just as important when managing stress. Consider this: A study from Johns Hopkins University demonstrated that emotional trauma can cause cardiomyopathy; it is commonly referred to as "broken heart syndrome," Many illnesses are caused or worsened by stress. Every thought has a corresponding physical reaction that can defend or attack our immune system. Is it any wonder that chronic stress can make us sick? Your thoughts matter. Your perspective matters.

*The most powerful pharmacy in the world is right between your ears.*

Mark Hyman, MD

## ONE MAN'S INSIGHT

The following excerpt is a powerful example of both the brain/body connection and stress reduction. Norman Cousins, editor of the Saturday Review for more than thirty years, was dying. Diagnosed with ankylosing spondylitis, a degenerative form of arthritis that causes the degradation of connective tissue in the spine, Cousins was given only a slim chance of recovery. With paralysis taking hold of his frail body, he checked himself out of the hospital and into a hotel. With the support of his physician, Dr. Cousins prescribed himself both high doses of vitamin C and laughter. Classic *Candid Camera* television episodes, Marx Brothers films, and humorous books became Cousins's antidote. "I made the joyous discovery that ten minutes of genuine belly laughter had an anesthetic effect and would give me at least two hours of pain-free sleep," he wrote in his 1979 bestselling book, *Anatomy of an Illness: As Perceived by the Patient*. "When the pain-killing effect of the laughter wore off, we would switch on the motion picture projector again, and not infrequently, it would lead to another pain-free interval." After each period of extended laughter, Cousins's sedimentation rate decreased, a sign of the body's increased ability to fight inflammation. "I was greatly elated by the discovery that there is a physiological basis for the ancient theory that laughter is good medicine," he noted.

*Hearty laughter is a good way to jog internally without having to go outdoors.*

Dr. Norman Cousins

Not only did Cousins go on to live twenty-six more years after his first diagnosis with this life-threatening disease, but he also created the Humor Research Task Force while an adjunct professor of psychiatry and biobehavioral science at the UCLA School of Medicine. His hunch was correct: The brain and body not only pay attention to each other, but also their special relationship absolutely depends on it.

*Laughter is a tranquilizer with no side effects.*

*Arnold Glasgow*

*The modern physician should know as much about emotions and thoughts as about disease symptoms and drugs. This approach would appear to hold more promise of cure than anything medicine has given us to date.*

*Hans Selye, MD (known as the "Father of Stress")*

*1907–1982*

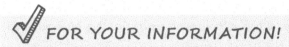

## FOR YOUR INFORMATION!

- Research on laughter indicates both short- and long-term benefits, such as producing a relaxed feeling, enhancing intake of oxygen-rich air, increasing endorphins, improving the immune response, relieving pain, and improving mood.

The challenges of life are ever-present and unyielding. By controlling your reaction to these events, you retain your power. Chronic stress demands your attention. Managing it accordingly brings ease and grace to your step. There are many effective tools to keep anxiety levels in check, but you must purposefully employ them. With so many tools at our fingertips, it is very possible to minimize our stress response with daily effort. I strongly encourage you to explore what fits your lifestyle and preference. Understanding that managing stress is not only a daily challenge but also a moment-to-moment one will yield a more fulfilled life.

*If we had no winter, the spring would not be so pleasant; if we did not sometimes taste adversity, prosperity, would not be so welcome.*

*Anne Broadstreet*

 REFLECTION

You might be a regular meditator, someone who used to meditate more frequently, or someone who has never meditated at all. It doesn't matter! Act now to better manage your stress and be better for your students. Become a Peak Performing Teacher. What are you committed to doing today, or if not today, then tomorrow? What form of stress management will you commit to? Can you commit to daily meditation, even if only fifteen minutes? What time of day? Can you commit to moments of purposeful mindfulness where you specifically focus on the moment during any number of activities? Can you take a few moments a day to breathe in a more focused and purposeful way? Are you willing to examine your thought processes and perspective and reframe them if need be? Planning to meditate or be mindful is one thing, but scheduling it makes it real! Please be detailed in your response.

Write your response here:

..................................................................................................................

..................................................................................................................

..................................................................................................................

..................................................................................................................

# STRESS IN THE CLASSROOM

If you are reading this book, you are all too familiar with the fact that students experience stress in school. According to www.mindfulschools.org:

- Nearly one in three adolescents will meet criteria for an anxiety disorder by the age of eighteen.

- In the United States, 46 percent of children have experienced at least one adverse childhood experience (ACE).

- On average, U.S. teens spend nine hours a day on digital entertainment.

- Nearly 40 percent of high school seniors report that they often feel lonely and left out.

The causes are many and often mirror life outside the classroom: stress at home, stress in social relationships, academic demands of school, bullying; there is no limit to what causes student stress. Often the brain is on full alert, which makes it difficult if not impossible to learn. According to Sousa (2017), the brain prioritizes incoming data on three levels: (1) survival, (2) emotion, and (3) the cognitive. The place where we need the brain to be to fully function and succeed in school is the last place it prioritizes. It's therefore imperative to recognize stress in students and help them manage it. You can safely assume some level of stress in your students every time you see them. It makes sense to help manage it. Here are some ideas:

- Keep your students moving. Physical activity is a stress and anxiety reducer. Many classroom-based physical activities force attention on the activity to perform it well. In other words, it forces you to pay attention to the moment and subsequently becomes a mindful activity. When you are forced to pay attention, especially to something that invigorates or causes laughter, stress momentarily vanishes providing some level of relief.

- Breathwork is a great stress reducer. It is mindful and can be meditative. Breath exercises can be used on their own or in combination with some progressive muscle relaxation, as I've previously described. When using breathing activities, have students try to keep their shoulders and chest as still as possible while focusing on belly breathing (making their stomachs rise and fall). As a former wind musician, I can tell you there is technique to this, but for our purposes here, having students focus on their bellies while breathing will be effective enough. It might help them to put a hand on their belly to make sure it is the part of the breathing apparatus that is rising and falling. If you are going to use the tensing of shoulders, arms, and fists along with the breath activity make sure students still use good breath form. I like for students to breathe in to a slow count of four, hold the breath for four counts, and finally exhale for four counts. Repeat up to five times. This can be done while being seated or standing.

- Use music. Music can be a very effective emotional state manager. It can excite, it can slow down, it can create joy and happiness, and it can also elicit a somber experience. It can touch on almost every emotion we can possibly experience, and it can also help reduce stress. Music can be part of a pleasant classroom environment and can be used as a background for many classroom experiences. Light classical music (think Mozart or Bach) can be used for background during academic work or cooperative activities. More upbeat music can be used with some physical activities. Calming and soothing new-age type of music can be used during stress reduction activities such as breath and progressive muscle relaxation activities.

Creating a classroom environment that helps students deal with their own stress is essential for every teacher. The more you manage it in your own life, the more you can help students manage theirs.

 # REFLECTION

How can you be more of a role model for your students regarding changing your mind and managing stress? What can you do to create a more stress-free classroom?

Write your response here:

.......................................................................................................................................................

.......................................................................................................................................................

.......................................................................................................................................................

.......................................................................................................................................................

# HABIT #3

. . . . . . . . . . . . . . . . . . . . . . . . . . . . .

## SHARPEN YOUR MENTAL FOCUS

### CREATING MISSION AND PURPOSE

# A MISSION STATEMENT IS NOT SOMETHING YOU WRITE OVERNIGHT, BUT FUNDAMENTALLY, YOUR MISSION STATEMENT BECOMES YOUR CONSTITUTION, THE SOLID EXPRESSION OF YOUR VISION AND VALUES. IT BECOMES THE CRITERION BY WHICH YOU MEASURE EVERYTHING ELSE IN YOUR LIFE.

STEPHEN COVEY

 IN THIS CHAPTER YOU'LL READ ABOUT

- How taking the time to develop a personal mission statement can lead to the pursuit of a life that captivates and motivates you both personally and professionally

- How a personal mission statement can help clarify your vision for the future, motivate you in achieving goals, and give you a values-based statement with which you can compare future decisions and choices

- Creating goals that can benefit our lives by creating the future in advance

- P.L.A.N., a broad-brush stroke approach to goal setting

- Outlining past successes, which can help people see when and how they reached goals in the past without having consciously mapped out the process

- The fundamentals of writing productive goals and creating effective action plans

# PART 1: THE PERSONAL MISSION STATEMENT

One topic that Tony Robbins discusses that has made a lasting impact on me is "designing a life versus making a living." This is a lofty ideal but one I've strived toward for the last three decades. An exemplary life, including being a successful teacher, that is both satisfying and joyful doesn't happen by accident. It is purpose- and values-driven. Purposefully creating the future beyond the next few days, weeks, and months requires a structure and vision that moves you in a direction of your desire and choosing. Taking the time to develop a personal mission statement can lead to a life that captivates and motivates you both personally and professionally, rather than leaving your life to fate or circumstance. This will help clarify your vision for the future, motivate you in achieving goals, and give you a values-based statement with which you can compare future decisions and choices. A personal mission statement can also help put you in the right state of mind as you begin each day in front of your students. To inspire them, you have to be inspired yourself. Remember the mirror? The reason for this book is to inspire you to live a more fulfilled life for your own benefit and in turn to inspire those around you including your students.

> If you are working on something exciting that you really care about, you don't have to be pushed. The vision pulls you through.
>
> Steve Jobs

Early in my professional career I created this personal mission statement:

> To inspire all people to be well, healthy, and motivated in order to live amazing, beautiful lives.

As you know, I come from a family of teachers. I was born to teach. I've been teaching adults for a long time. It comes naturally to me, and I'm comfortable doing it, whether I'm in front of seven wellness champions in a Boston Public School copy room or giving a keynote address in front of a thousand teachers in Manilla. My mission helps make my purpose crystal clear. It doesn't matter if I'm teaching about physical activity, wellness, motivation, brain-compatible methods, or differentiated instruction: I'm trying to inspire my audience to raise their level of living, giving, and teaching. My mission inspires me through the principles I prioritize. I've been asked to do many different things throughout my career. When I've said no to a book, project, or professional development experience, it's often because it didn't align with my mission. That clarity and vision is a gift. My personal mission statement gives me greater confidence and less stress during the decision-making process.

> Clarity of vision creates clarity of priorities.
>
> John C. Maxwell

## HERE ARE THE PERSONAL MISSION STATEMENTS OF A FEW PEOPLE WHO YOU MIGHT RECOGNIZE:

### Oprah Winfrey

To be a teacher. And to be known for inspiring my students to be more than they thought they could be.

### Richard Branson

To have fun in my journey through life and learn from my mistakes.

### Mahatma Gandhi

I shall not fear anyone on Earth. I shall fear only God. I shall not bear ill will toward anyone. I shall not submit to injustice from anyone. I shall conquer untruth by truth. And in resisting untruth, I shall put up with all suffering.

### Elon Musk

If something is important enough you should try, even if the probable outcome is failure.

### Walt Disney

To make people happy.

### Tony Robbins

To humbly serve our Lord by being a loving, playful, powerful, and passionate example of the absolute joy that is available to us the moment we rejoice in God's gifts and sincerely love and serve all his creations.

### Amanda Steinberg (founder of Daily Worth)

To use my gifts of intelligence, charisma, and serial optimism to cultivate the self-worth and net-worth of women around the world.

## CREATING YOUR PERSONAL MISSION STATEMENT

Creating a personal mission statement takes time, effort, and a good amount of reflection. You are going to need a process of effective self-examination that allows your brain to get into a reflective mindset and mood. I would recommend you find a quiet, comfortable space in which to work. Turn off your phone. Writing your mission statement is a deep reflection of your values and priorities, so you want to minimize distractions. The purpose of answering the following prompts and questions is to tease out and think about what you prioritize, value, hope for, and want to achieve and impact.

To begin the process, identify the characteristics of your favorite teacher; the one whose class you looked forward to, the one who inspired you, and quite possibly the one who inspired you to be a teacher.

List the characteristics here:

..................................................................................................................................

..................................................................................................................................

..................................................................................................................................

What was the classroom environment of this teacher like? How did you feel when you were in this class with this teacher?

..................................................................................................................................

..................................................................................................................................

..................................................................................................................................

Why did you want to become a teacher? Does this answer reflect your current situation? Is your teaching career what you'd hoped it would be?

..................................................................................................................................

..................................................................................................................................

..................................................................................................................................

Now focus on a time where you really made a difference in a student's life. It could have been in the classroom, in a coaching arena, or some other scenario where you had the ability to impact a child's life. Write your answer briefly here:

..................................................................................................................................

..................................................................................................................................

..................................................................................................................................

Three former students have been asked to be on a podcast regarding your influence on their lives. In a few sentences, what would they say?

..................................................................................................................................

..................................................................................................................................

..................................................................................................................................

What strengths, skills, and/or abilities do you have that bring out the best in you or can put you in a state of flow?

..................................................................................................................................

..................................................................................................................................

..................................................................................................................................

What inspires you?

.......................................................................................................................................
.......................................................................................................................................
.......................................................................................................................................

When you are not in the classroom, what do you love to do?

.......................................................................................................................................
.......................................................................................................................................
.......................................................................................................................................

What stirs your passions?

.......................................................................................................................................
.......................................................................................................................................
.......................................................................................................................................

Imagine the best version of yourself. What does it look like?

.......................................................................................................................................
.......................................................................................................................................
.......................................................................................................................................

If you could have dinner with any one person, who would it be? Why? What would you discuss?

.......................................................................................................................................
.......................................................................................................................................
.......................................................................................................................................

What values guide your life? Are there rules or personal promises against which you compare your actions?

.......................................................................................................................................
.......................................................................................................................................
.......................................................................................................................................

What thing most represents you?

..............................................................................................................

..............................................................................................................

..............................................................................................................

Who has had the most impact on your growth and development? Why?

..............................................................................................................

..............................................................................................................

..............................................................................................................

At the close of your teaching career, what would you have others think about your impact? What would they say?

..............................................................................................................

..............................................................................................................

..............................................................................................................

What is the ultimate goal for your life?

..............................................................................................................

..............................................................................................................

..............................................................................................................

## PERSONAL MISSION STATEMENT ROUGH DRAFT

In the space below create a rough draft based on the answers you have just given. You might use some of the previously listed mission statements as a guide, or you might reflect on a favorite quote or two. Johnny Mercer says, "You must write for the wastebasket." I think about that quote every time I sit down to write. I know I must simply lean in and start writing. I already know that it's going to be far from perfect but provides a good starting point. And, if it helps, I always do a quick visualization of a successful writing process before I begin. Simply allow your thoughts to flow without worrying about proper writing technique or grammar. Get your thoughts on paper. What is your mission?

..............................................................................................................

..............................................................................................................

..............................................................................................................

..............................................................................................................

## COMPLETED MISSION STATEMENT

Now that your rough draft is complete, it's time to write out your completed personal mission statement:

...................................................................................................................

...................................................................................................................

...................................................................................................................

...................................................................................................................

...................................................................................................................

...................................................................................................................

...................................................................................................................

...................................................................................................................

...................................................................................................................

...................................................................................................................

...................................................................................................................

My personal mission statement is framed and hanging in my office. It's important to make it visible in multiple places. You've taken the time to deeply reflect on the creation of a statement that will hopefully inspire you. Read and reflect on it often!

> *Outstanding people have one thing in common: an absolute sense of mission.*
>
> Zig Ziglar

## PART 2: SETTING GOALS

> *If you want to be happy, set a goal that commands your thoughts, liberates your energy, and inspires your hopes.*
>
> Andrew Carnegie

Now that you've created a personal mission statement, it becomes easier to create goals and plans of action that align with your values, vision, and purpose. Let's revisit my participation in the Broad Street Run, a ten-mile road race in the city of Philadelphia, which I referenced in Chapter 1. When I started my journey, I had no idea how profoundly it would impact my life. At this point, I had already designed a graduate course on staff and student motivation, including goal setting, and I knew that I needed to create a goal around this race. Looking back at how much momentum it created in my life and what an undertaking it was at forty-three years of age, it was a very smart decision. We all have things we want to achieve. Setting goals can get us there more predictably and more quickly. No part of my goal had to do with how fast I would run the race but rather with finishing it! Here's the goal I mapped out:

**Goal:** By May 3, 2009, at 8:00 a.m. I will be able to run 10 miles without stopping.

**Why?** Because I want to finish the Broad Street Run with my friends, create a more healthful way of life, and experience the positive emotions this accomplishment will bring with it.

**Action Plan:**

- Purchase a book that specifically deals with beginning runners and read it in its entirety.
- Buy proper running shoes.
- Recruit the help of a coach/friend/partner.
- Run 4 1/2 miles within two days and journal how it felt.
- Run three times weekly on the same days each week at a time when my schedule allows.
- Increase the distance by one mile every two weeks until I reach ten miles.
- Reach my goal in plenty of time.
- Feel great about my new endurance and health level, appreciate all other benefits, and increase the distance.

**Immediate Action(s):** Register for the race, and buy the book.

**Resource Individual:** My running coach/partner

The result of achieving this goal was almost too good to be true. The emotions of joy, gratitude, accomplishment, and satisfaction flooded through me just like I had imagined. As you have already read, I credit this event with fueling me with the energy and motivation that led to the publication of my first book, which was a game-changer for me professionally and personally. I also lost a good amount of weight, felt fit, and could roll out of bed and run six or seven miles as an afterthought. Not only did I exceed my goal of running ten miles, but I was also running eleven miles several times a week and began to set my sights on longer races. Another important result of this goal for me personally was the entire weekend celebration with great friends. We made a weekend of it in Philadelphia including a delicious carb-loading Italian meal in Rittenhouse Square the night before the race. I got to achieve all of this in a social setting, which is important to me.

> Goals. There's no telling what you can do when you get inspired by them. There's no telling what you can do when you believe in them. And there's no telling what will happen when you act upon them.
>
> Jim Rohn

For me personally, there are four things that I know about setting goals for my life:

1. They give my brain focus. Goals tell my brain "I'm here, and I want to be there." The gap that exists between where I am and where I want to be creates a good

pressure, brings the blurred into focus, creates energy and effort, and fuels motivation. Going from four miles to eleven miles in thirteen weeks is intense but possible. Our goals need to energize us because of their difficulty but not defeat us from the outset because they are completely out of reach.

2. It gives me a plan that I can focus on. Good things have a better chance of happening when you plan with specificity and detail. It also provides a framework for collecting data as to whether I'm moving closer to my goal or whether I need to re-examine my plan to make better progress. I tracked my miles each time I ran to make sure I was making progress toward my ten-mile goal. If I had to do a shorter run, I simply upped the intensity through speed and/or geography.

3. Setting goals gives me an opportunity to examine what things in my life push me toward the achievement of my goals and what things in my life push me away from the achievement of my goals. It forces me to examine what is good for my life and what it is that might hold it back. I learned through this process that being more organized with my time pushes me closer to my goals. I've also learned how to weave my goals into my social life, such as working out with a friend or turning an activity into a more social event by inviting friends to join me in the gym or to go mountain biking.

4. They help me to identify the emotions around "my why." Emotions run our lives. We are our emotions. If I can channel that energy for a specific purpose, I have a much better chance of succeeding. Honestly, the main emotion around the Broad Street Run was not getting into great shape, losing weight, or being able to run ten miles without stopping. It was the fact that I wanted to enjoy this event with my friends. That's initially why I raised my hand and said, "I'm in."

## FOR YOUR INFORMATION!

According to vanSonnenberg (2011), research on goal setting indicates that the following:

- Self-confidence, self-esteem, and motivation are all linked to goal setting.
- Writing down goals enhances goal achievement.
- Setting more difficult goals leads to greater achievement.
- The more specific a goal is written the more performance can be measured.
- The combination of specificity and difficulty leads to greater performance.
- People are more committed to goals when they find them both to be important (What is your why?) and attainable.
- Feedback showing progress toward goal attainment makes goal setting more effective.
- And, according to Klein et al. (2020), reporting action plan progress with someone whose opinion they respect significantly enhances the likelihood of goal achievement. Making yourself accountable to another could make a measurable difference.

If you are determined to follow through, setting goals will not disappoint. Set a goal, create an action plan, check frequently to see whether it's working, and if it's not, move to Plan B. If Plan B doesn't work, move to Plan C, and so on. If you just keep moving forward with action, you'll eventually get it right. The problem is that very few people check frequently for progress, and fewer still adjust their action plan. To make this point to graduate education students, I'll often ask them to get into groups of five or six, line up side by side and arm in arm. The goal is simple: to walk ten to fifteen feet while making sure their ankles always touch. It is much harder than it sounds. It will take a plan, communication, coordination, and synergy. I have each group document their efforts. Once the fun is had, I debrief the activity by asking what individual groups used as a process. It usually looks something like this:

Step 1—Group members reflected upon the goal of walking ten to fifteen feet without losing touch with the ankle next to them.

Step 2—Plans of action were created as they tried the process.

Step 3—They noticed whether it was working or not.

Step 4—They changed their approach until they achieved their goal.

The result is something I call **P.L.A.N.** To be very succinct, here is the four-step success formula for change and achievement and reaching goals. It is foolproof if you'll follow through:

**P**lan your vision, and begin with the end goal or desired outcome. In other words, you must set goals. To get where you're going, setting goals becomes essential because it creates pressure. It not only gives your brain something to focus on but also creates a sense of "I'm here and want to be there." As stated previously, this creates a good pressure, which gives your brain a map and helps you to take action toward the attainment of a particular goal.

**L**ist your actions or create an action plan. Many people set goals, even write them down, but fail to create a plan of action that is specific and absolutely necessary for achievement. An action plan becomes a map for achievement. It lets our brain know exactly what to do to reach our goal. Creating a goal without an action plan is like piloting a flight to a new destination without GPS.

**A**ssess the outcomes or notice whether the plan is working or not! Whatever your goal is, it's very important to be aware of whether you're moving closer to your goal or further away. If you have made it to the point of creating an action plan, it is important to continually check your progress. We must ask ourselves, "Am I being effective?"

If your plan is not working, determine a **N**ew approach. It can be frightening to create goals because you might fail! Failure is scary, but it doesn't have to be as it can be a great teacher. When anyone sets a goal, he or she is taking a risk. They are putting themselves out there by telling the world, or just themselves, that they want to achieve this goal. Because of this, people often quit if their plan does not work out. This requires a change in perspective! If a plan doesn't work, let it be a teacher! Now you know what doesn't work! It's a free education. Now it's time to change your approach, and if that doesn't work, change it again, and if that doesn't work, then change it again! You'll eventually get it right!

Essentially that is the four-step process for the successful achievement of a goal; easier said than done. Let's take a look at a real-life example:

Suppose someone had a goal of losing ten lbs. The process might look like this:

1. (P) Create a very specific goal: In eight weeks, by June 12, 2025, I will lose ten lbs. This tells my brain exactly what the plan is.

2. (L) The action plan might include the following:

   - I will clean out my pantry and refrigerator of all unhealthy and processed foods (If you can't grow it, don't eat it).

   - I will replace unhealthy processed foods with fresh fruits, nuts, and vegetables.

   - I will plan out my entire week of meals and shop and prepare the food each Sunday.

     - I will eat four small meals per day that always include fresh fruit or vegetables. If I eat a lean protein, it will be the size of a deck of cards or the palm of my hand.

   - I will drink plenty of water every day.

   - I will eliminate all sweets, treats, and candy from my diet.

   - I will weigh myself each Saturday morning to see if I'm making progress toward my goal.

   - I will feel great and move toward eating as a lifestyle change!

3. (A) Is the plan working? Have I completed each one of the steps? There is a lot that could go right in this plan, and there is a lot that could go wrong. Getting on the scale each Saturday morning gives me an opportunity to see if my plan is working or not. If I wait until the halfway point (four weeks) to get on the scale and haven't made any progress toward my goal, I could risk losing significant amounts of motivation to continue. This is why short-term goals can be very effective. If I'm making progress toward my goal each week, I feel great about continuing. If I haven't lost any weight after Week 1, I can easily adjust what I'm doing because I am not very far into the process. After one week, all is not lost, and I'm more motivated to adjust and move forward.

4. (N) What do I need to adjust to make this plan work, or do I need to create another plan? Did I find myself eating foods that don't contribute toward my goal? Do I need to think in more broad terms and add exercise to my plan? Are my portion sizes too big? The assessment of our progress gives us an opportunity to create a new approach if necessary.

*By recording your dreams and goals on paper, you set in motion the process of becoming the person you most want to be. Put your future in good hands—your own.*

*Mark Victor Hansen*

# REFLECTION

As a way to make this process more real, I will often ask graduate students to outline a past success. We all have them. Examining them in terms of P.L.A.N. can be an eye-opener for future goal setting.

Answer the following set of questions:

What success in your life was once only a dream; something that went from a thought to reality? When did it become a definite idea?

..........................................................................................................................

..........................................................................................................................

..........................................................................................................................

Next, create a list of the steps it took to attain your goal.

..........................................................................................................................

..........................................................................................................................

..........................................................................................................................

Next, reflect on the following questions:

How long did the process take?

..........................................................................................................................

..........................................................................................................................

..........................................................................................................................

Was there a clear path available from thought to fruition?

..........................................................................................................................

..........................................................................................................................

..........................................................................................................................

Were there obstacles along the way? If so, how were they overcome?

..........................................................................................................................

..........................................................................................................................

..........................................................................................................................

Was there any doubt in your mind as to the outcome?

..........................................................................................................................

..........................................................................................................................

..........................................................................................................................

What most people will have outlined is a simple formula for success:

Start with the end goal in mind—create an action plan—assess if what you are doing is working—if not. change your approach. Many times, the process of achieving this past success could have been streamlined and become more efficient if we had created a written plan. If you are reading this book, you are a quite capable human being. You are also entrusted with our greatest resource—children. You are all capable of almost anything you want to achieve. Goal setting makes this process more probable and creates more of a straight line from where you are to where you want to be.

## UNDERSTANDING THE DIFFERENCE BETWEEN A GOOD IDEA AND WRITING A GOAL

"I want to lose weight" is a good idea. "I will weigh 165 lbs. by October 1 at 5 p.m." is a very detailed and specific goal. Just like our previous discussion about gratitude, the more granular and specific you can be with goal setting, the more guidance your brain has to move forward, and the more you will be inspired to work toward it. The goal of losing weight is admirable but difficult to measure effectively. If we need to regularly assess moving toward our goal, the second way it is written is much more effective. It tells me exactly what and by when. Here are a few more examples of good ideas versus specific, measurable goals:

> I would like to move from renting to purchasing a home.
>
> vs.
>
> I will own a home in Spring Lake, NJ by 1:00 p.m. on March 31, 2024.
>
> or
>
> I would like to get a master's degree.
>
> vs.
>
> I will earn a master's degree in education by June 1st, 2024.

Being specific about how much time is allotted for completion is critical to the goal-setting process. It gives the brain something specific to focus on and moves it to action. It also creates that positive pressure I spoke about earlier. Pressure can be used to one's own great advantage. Pressure helps "shoulds" become "musts"! By all means. make sure your goals inspire you! They must be lofty but realistic at the same time. If someone wants to lose 25 lbs. in two weeks, it is probably not realistic, or attainable, for most, nor is it healthy. A better time frame would be over the course of three months. I am fifty-five years old during the writing of this book, and I love professional baseball, but I have neither the talent, desire, nor the physical ability to make a career playing major league baseball. It's lofty but not realistic. This example is a little over the top, but you see my point. Here are some other things to consider when setting goals:

1. Make sure the goal you are working for is something you really want, not just something that sounds good. Our desires change over time. Something that looks appealing to have or achieve may not be something we really want. From an emotional standpoint the more we really want something the more we are likely to go get it.

2. Make sure your goal is high enough. Your goals need to challenge and inspire you. This is a fine balance between being too easy and so difficult the goal becomes unattainable.

3. Write your goal out in complete detail. The more specific a goal is written, the better a blueprint the brain must focus on moving closer to the goal in an efficient way.

4. Do something immediately that moves you closer toward achieving it. Writing out your goal creates momentum, and you want to sustain that momentum with immediate action. If you have set a financial goal one immediate action might be to make an appointment with a financial advisor.

5. Create an action plan to support your goal. Writing out your goal in detail and even understanding why you want to achieve it are great first steps. but failing to create a detailed plan will most likely result in failure. Give your brain a chance with a detailed plan that you can refer to, to see if you are making positive progress.

6. Find a resource individual who can help you achieve your goal or simply be the one you make progress reports to.

Goal setting can suffer from familiarity. People hear and learn about setting goals all the time. but they often don't do it, or if they do, they don't do it effectively. Goal setting is one of those life fundamentals that can raise our level of living. The best in the world, at whatever it is, practice fundamentals each day. Goal setting is in that category and needs attention paid to it often. This begs an essential question: What do you want (starting with the end goal in mind)? With the answer to that question, you begin to concretize desire and begin making it real. Once the definition is established, define the emotion behind the goal; behind answering the question of "why?" Finding reasons to achieve goals makes the process that much more powerful. When the reasons become powerful enough. the brain will move everything into action. which provides an opportunity to figure out how to accomplish the goal.

Now, it's your turn. Before writing specific goals, take a few minutes for each area that I'm going to ask you to write a goal (personal, professional, and fun), and brainstorm a dream list of everything you want for that particular area. Go crazy! Big lives are started with big thoughts and dreams! You may want to be in the best shape of your life, become a superintendent of schools, and vacation in Hawaii once a year. I don't know what the "what" is for you, but think big!

## PERSONAL DEVELOPMENT BRAINSTORMING IDEAS

..............................................................................................................................

..............................................................................................................................

..............................................................................................................................

..............................................................................................................................

From your brainstormed list identify one personal development goal, and write a few sentences stating why you are dedicated to achieving it.

..............................................................................................................................

..............................................................................................................................

..............................................................................................................................

..............................................................................................................................

## PROFESSIONAL DEVELOPMENT BRAINSTORMING IDEAS

..................................................................................................................

..................................................................................................................

..................................................................................................................

..................................................................................................................

..................................................................................................................

From your brainstormed list identify one professional development goal, and write a few sentences stating why you are dedicated to achieving it.

..................................................................................................................

..................................................................................................................

..................................................................................................................

..................................................................................................................

..................................................................................................................

## JUST FOR FUN BRAINSTORMING IDEAS

..................................................................................................................

..................................................................................................................

..................................................................................................................

..................................................................................................................

From your brainstormed list identify one just for fun goal, and write a few sentences stating why you are dedicated to achieving it.

..................................................................................................................

..................................................................................................................

..................................................................................................................

..................................................................................................................

## CREATING THE FUTURE NOW

*List One Personal Development Goal.* Underneath your goal, list why you are committed to its achievement in the timeline described. Next, create an action plan for the goal. Also, list an immediate action you can take today, and identify someone who can help you toward its attainment.

Specific Goal and Time Frame:

..............................................................................................................................

Why?

..............................................................................................................................

Action Plan:

..............................................................................................................................

Immediate Action:

..............................................................................................................................

..............................................................................................................................

Resource Individual:

..............................................................................................................................

..............................................................................................................................

*List One Professional Development Goal.* Underneath your goal, list why you are committed to its achievement in the timeline described. Next, create an action plan for your goal. Also, list an immediate action you can take today, and identify someone who can help you toward its attainment.

Specific Goal and Time Frame:

..............................................................................................................................

Why?

..............................................................................................................................

Action Plan:

..............................................................................................................................

..............................................................................................................................

Immediate Action:

..............................................................................................................................

..............................................................................................................................

Resource Individual:

..............................................................................................................................

*List One Personal "Just for Fun" Goal.* Underneath your goal, list why you are committed to its achievement in the timeline described. Next, create an action plan for your goal. Also, list an immediate action you can take today, and identify someone who can help you toward its attainment.

Specific Goal and Time Frame:

..............................................................................................................................

Why?

..............................................................................................................................

Action Plan:

...................................................................................................................................

...................................................................................................................................

Immediate Action:

...................................................................................................................................

...................................................................................................................................

Resource Individual:

...................................................................................................................................

The best time to P.L.A.N. the next year of your life is now. Which goal will you be setting out to achieve first? What are you going to do today to move toward it becoming a reality?

*Our goals can only be reached through a vehicle of a plan, in which we must vigorously act. There is no other route to success.*

Pablo Picasso

## CREATING A TRANSFORMATIONAL GOAL

Hopefully you've just written down and committed to three different short-term goals—one personal development goal, one professional development goal, and one "I just want to have a fun goal." Now, I'd like you to think about creating a breakthrough, or transformational goal, as I like to call them. These types of goals can transform people's lives, like losing fifty pounds, writing a book, making a movie, being a guest on a television show, creating a website, getting another degree, or starting a business. Defining breakthrough or transformational depends on personal perspective. Pursuing goals usually means step-by-step changes in our lives. It's like bunting your way on base and stealing every other bag until you've made your way home. But what if you could hit a home run or a grand slam? That could mean a dramatic change in your life! I know many teachers who've earned a master's degree or a doctorate, who've become supervisors and administrators, earned their National Board Certification, or have become a leader in a union or professional organization. I've also known teachers who have become bloggers, started their own podcasts, and even founded their own businesses! Wouldn't these more transformational goals be worth pursuing? I personally know dozens of teachers who set out to become graduate-level instructors. The process is intense but one that creates professional opportunity like conference presentations and keynotes, authoring books, and creating new levels of influence in their profession and back in their school districts. It also can provide an unprecedented change in income level. Most importantly, all these examples I'm citing can create new opportunities and take life to another level. As you work on your transformational goal, keep in mind these three things that I learned as I pursued my life's work:

It is never too late in life to pursue and achieve dreams and goals!

I am capable of much more than I ever knew or expected of myself!

I can achieve anything I put my mind to!

What is your transformational goal (Think big!)? Write it here:

.........................................................................................................................................

.........................................................................................................................................

.........................................................................................................................................

.........................................................................................................................................

You know the next steps! List your actions, assess the outcomes, and adjust if necessary. And before getting started, determine your why, find a friend to lean on, and take immediate action! Good luck!

*The achievement of your goal is assured the moment you commit yourself to it.*

Mack R. Douglas

## THE ROCKING CHAIR TEST

At this point, I ask you to take the rocking chair test. I certainly didn't invent this well-known and simple test, but I have used it personally many times. It allows us to evaluate whether or not we really want to set out to achieve something. By the end of this chapter, you've had the opportunity to create four goals—three detailed ones and the more general breakthrough goal. Choose one to reflect upon. Close your eyes, and imagine you are sitting on a rocking chair near the end of your life. Moving back and forth in the chair and reflecting upon your life, imagine *not* having reached that particular goal. How does that make you feel? How did this affect the rest of your life? Your family's lives? The people's lives you did not touch? Now imagine you achieved your goal! How did the rest of your life change? How did it affect your future? Your family's future? How did it have a ripple effect in your life and the lives of others? What is your life now like because you accomplished this goal? How does that feel? At its core, it's a pain/pleasure test. Does the pain of not having achieved your goal outweigh the pleasure of not having to do the work it required? Did the pleasure of achieving this goal outweigh the pain of having to have earned it through discipline and hard work? The answer might surprise—and will inform—you.

## GOAL SETTING IN THE CLASSROOM

Schools and classrooms are no strangers to goal setting. As with adults, goal setting helps students focus on a particular intention, influence persistence and resolve, and create energy and motivation. Their use in schools can have a positive influence on student outcomes and school culture. The key to it is to make goal setting as second nature as sharpening a pencil. The more you set goals for your own life, the more easily you'll be able to facilitate them with your students. When students are taught how to properly set goals, create action plans, check for progress and recalibrate as necessary, goal setting can be a very effective tool in an academic or extracurricular setting. Setting goals will also help students to become more deeply involved in, and directing, their own learning.

Specific action plans can also make the connection between immediate action steps and future goal attainment. All the same rules apply—goals need to be written in a very specific way that is sensitive to time and challenge.

I'm also going to suggest that goals be written for the short term, meaning achievement of a goal or falling short of a goal should be determined after a short time period such as a week. I might have a goal for getting a semester grade of "A" in a particular class. If halfway through the marking period I'm not even close to an A, my motivation levels will fall considerably. But if I break my goals down into one-week goals and plans of action I can assess after a very short period of time. After one week, if I've hit my goal, I can celebrate. This creates more motivation to succeed the following week. If I fail to reach my goal, I'm not so far into the process that I lose my momentum. I just need to assess what I've done and make the necessary changes. Students need to learn how to break things down into smaller tasks to prevent overwhelm and avoidance of larger tasks.

Feedback is critical to a successful goal journey. Goal achievement is much more difficult without it. And remember, the research says that when we share our goals and progress with someone else, we are more likely to attain them. Maybe your students have a goal-setting partner to make the process more fun and realistic. The priority becomes making kids feel some measure of success so they can build on it. We want students to achieve goals and experience success, so they build confidence in order to maintain motivation and be willing to keep reaching higher. Success builds on itself, and the struggle can be a great teacher. We also want them to view failure as a teacher; something normal that's part of the process of growth and achievement.

The fundamentals of goal setting are similar in any situation but can be expressed in many different ways. You may be a high school physics teacher or a kindergarten teacher. Goals can be effective in both situations but will be expressed and experienced very differently. If possible, tap into students' interests. Interest is a directive force and a very powerful motivator. If goal setting success is initially experienced through an interest, it could lead to greater willingness to participate in goal setting when the subject might not be as interesting. One of the most critical elements in student motivation and achievement is one's belief in his or her own abilities to achieve. It is quite possible that a fine-tuned goal-setting process can lead to greater belief in a student's own abilities.

# REFLECTION

The following questions may help to clarify your own intentions for using goal setting with your students.

How often do you teach students to set specific goals including an action plan?

..............................................................................................................................

..............................................................................................................................

..............................................................................................................................

..............................................................................................................................

..............................................................................................................................

Have you missed opportunities to use goal-setting techniques with your students in content area instruction?

........................................................................................................................................

........................................................................................................................................

........................................................................................................................................

........................................................................................................................................

What obstacles could arise as you help students formulate goals?

........................................................................................................................................

........................................................................................................................................

........................................................................................................................................

........................................................................................................................................

What are some other ideas you could use with your students related to goal setting?

........................................................................................................................................

........................................................................................................................................

........................................................................................................................................

........................................................................................................................................

How could you integrate goal setting into your next unit? When will you do it?

........................................................................................................................................

........................................................................................................................................

........................................................................................................................................

........................................................................................................................................

How could you monitor progress by having students revisit goals throughout the unit?

........................................................................................................................................

........................................................................................................................................

........................................................................................................................................

........................................................................................................................................

........................................................................................................................................

How could you help students reflect on their goals, celebrate their achievements, and set new goals for upcoming units?

...........................................................................................................................................

...........................................................................................................................................

...........................................................................................................................................

...........................................................................................................................................

...........................................................................................................................................

*All successful people have a goal. No one can get anywhere unless he knows where he wants to go and what he wants to be or do.*

*Norman Vincent Peale*

# HABIT #4

## POWER UP GRATITUDE

# I AM HAPPY BECAUSE I'M GRATEFUL. I CHOOSE TO BE GRATEFUL. THAT GRATITUDE ALLOWS ME TO BE HAPPY.

WILL ARNETT

 IN THIS CHAPTER YOU'LL READ ABOUT

- Research that shows that practicing gratitude can have many benefits, including becoming happier, healthier, more mentally resilient, and at lower risk for developing depression and anxiety

- A business success whose underlying premise is practicing gratitude

- Four ways to create meaningful and rich gratitude experiences every day through experience and writing

- How each day brings a new opportunity to mine for gratefulness and put a frame on—or how you choose to look at things in—every situation

- Several ways to increase gratefulness through activities like gratitude journaling, writing thank-you notes, gratitude letters, and gratitude mining

- How gratitude can benefit the students in your classroom

## If you could purposefully choose more happiness and well-being, would you?

If research, anecdotes, and real-life experience demonstrated that it is immediately possible to become happier and more well through a certain type of action, would you stop what you are doing and do it? Better yet, if you could achieve a greater level of happiness and well-being without grand effort and it cost nothing to do, would you?

*I don't have to chase extraordinary moments to find happiness—it's right in front of me if I'm paying attention and practicing gratitude.*

Brene Brown

Creating a physical life requires some level of exertion through various types of exercise, which for some people could create barriers to success. Managing stress for the long haul can also take time to learn specific techniques such as meditation or progressive muscle relaxation. But research shows that you can experience a happiness response right away through the practice of gratitude. Of all the habits I will suggest to you in this book, practicing gratitude is the simplest (and the least expensive—free!!!). It requires very little from you, and the return has extraordinary possibilities. It's like investing $10 in the stock market and getting a $100,000 return almost immediately.

*Gratitude is not only the greatest of virtues, but the parent of all others.*

Marcus Tullius Cicero

I'm not suggesting that practicing gratitude every so often is going to change your life. I'm asking you to create a new or more extensive habit than that, and for a small amount of effort on a consistent basis the return can be profound.

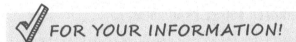 FOR YOUR INFORMATION!

According to Craig (2021) research indicates the following:

- Turning your outlook to one of gratitude can increase happiness due to experiencing and taking pleasure from positive emotions.
- Individuals who are grateful exercise more regularly, experience fewer aches and pains, and are more likely to take care of their health.
- Being thankful puts you at lower risk for depression, anxiety, and alcohol and drug dependence.
- Gratitude is associated with a high satisfaction in life and a greater sense of meaning and purpose.
- Grateful people are more sensitive, empathetic, have increased self-esteem, and are less likely to seek revenge.
- Gratitude creates an increase in mental resilience and an easement of symptoms from posttraumatic stress disorder (PTSD).
- Gratitude leads to improved sleep quality.
- Gratitude can cause strengthened relationship connection and satisfaction.

# WHO DOESN'T WANT THESE BENEFITS FOR SO VERY LITTLE EFFORT?

 REFLECTION

There is no better time than now to begin practicing gratitude. Who are you grateful for? Why? Be as specific as possible! Even better, tell that person as soon as possible!

Write your response here:

........................................................................................................................

........................................................................................................................

........................................................................................................................

Focusing only on one thing, what are you grateful for? Why? Be as specific as possible!

Write your response here:

........................................................................................................................

........................................................................................................................

........................................................................................................................

There is some research to suggest that practicing gratitude on a weekly basis can be more effective than daily. People sometimes find it difficult to identify that much to be grateful for, and daily practice can become mundane. I have never had this problem. I tend to practice gratitude whenever I can, and that means several times a day. I know this is not for everyone. I simply like the way it makes me feel. I lean on gratitude constantly to manage my own state. When I'm stressed? I get grateful. When I'm scared? I get grateful. When I'm tense? I get grateful. When I'm angry? I get grateful. This practice changes how I feel instantly. It might be a bit pollyannish, but it works for me. Not all situations can be improved quickly by practicing gratefulness, but many can. When I show gratitude for that which scares, ails, or haunts me, it allows for a change in perspective. That is one of the great blessings that practicing gratefulness can bring. I cannot imagine starting my day without practicing gratefulness. It's routine for me. It sets the right mindset so I can approach the day more successfully.

> When we focus on our gratitude, the tide of disappointment goes out and the tide of love rushes in.
>
> Kristin Armstrong

In his TED Talk with almost three million views, "Want to be happy? Be Grateful" David Steindl-Rast (2013) says it this way:

We all want to be happy. When we are happy, we are grateful. Is it really the happy people that are grateful? But think again. Is it really the happy people that are grateful? We all know quite a number of people who have everything that it would take to be happy and they are not happy because they want something else or they want more of the same. And we all know people who have lots of misfortune . . . and they are deeply happy. They radiate happiness. Why? Because they are grateful. It's not happiness that makes us grateful, it's gratefulness that makes us happy.

# IN THE BUSINESS OF GRATITUDE

I have met many kind, grateful people in my life, but none match the level of gratitude practiced by entrepreneur Eric Savage. Eric brought his gratefulness to work. Eric brought gratitude to his employees and customers. It is so unique, groundbreaking, and impressive that I reached out to him to share his story—an entrepreneur who founded a business on gratitude—a "Life Improvement Business." Eric's vision reminds me of the following quote by Jen Sincero:

> Gratitude is one of the strongest and most transformative states of being. It shifts your perspective from lack to abundance and allows you to focus on the good in your life, which in turn pulls more goodness into your reality.

Eric wanted his employees, and more importantly, his customers, to have this type of experience within his business—car dealerships. Eric's personal and business philosophy, vision, and intention is to improve lives. In his words, "If we really believe that we are here to improve the lives of others, there needs to be a logic that creates that possibility, 'gates' that need to be passed through in order for that to happen." As I listened to Eric talk, I not only heard many valuable offerings for any individual person but also began noticing parallels and applications for schools. While I ask you to read the following excerpt as a way to more deeply understand how it might be possible for gratitude to play out in your own life, I would also ask you to look for parallels that could be useful in the classroom. Because if gratitude can create more happiness, health, empathy, and resilience and less aggression, depression, and anxiety, who doesn't want that in their classroom?

I asked very little of Eric. Rather, like a modern-day philosopher, Eric instinctually knew what I needed to hear. I can safely say that after transcribing the interview, the information became even more clear and profound.

And so, Eric began . . .

There is only one way to improve a life, and that is to create value: Human value that has a heart attached to it; not commercial value that has a dollar sign attached to it. It's about what we are willing to give of ourselves and transfer to other people. The only way to improve a human life, to create human value, has more to do with what is happening in here (Eric points to his chest) and less to do with what is happening in a wallet. Life improvement is the natural result of creating human value. How do we create human value? When we are good givers. Imagine a continuum that exists where one extreme is "giving," and the other extreme is "getting." Where we position ourselves on this continuum is the key to creating human value. Our actions, behaviors, and words determine how far we are on the giving side of the continuum. When we are positioned between the extreme end of the "giving" side of the continuum and the person with whom we are transacting, then the delta we create between ourselves and that person is the size of the human value we create. If I am one inch closer to the giving side than they are, I create a small space and relatively small human value between the two of us, but if I move ten more feet toward the giving side, I now create much more value for the other person. By creating more human value I am improving lives.

It begs the questions:

> Aren't all teachers in the business of creating human value? In the life improvement business?

How do I then make myself a good giver? How do I move myself more to the "giving" side of the continuum with frequency and potency? The answer is that there are other parallel continuums: abundance and scarcity, and love and fear. When I am an abundant person giving is easy. It's not even hard. It's not sacrificial, it's just natural.

Eric goes on to ask me:

"Did you ever have a tomato garden?"

"No."

"Did you ever have a neighbor with a tomato garden?"

"Yes."

"Did you end up with tomatoes?"

"Yes."

"Why?"

"Because they wanted to give me tomatoes?" I ask. "Tomatoes grow, and my neighbors want to enrich my life, so they give me tomatoes."

"It's much more basic than that. It's because they have too many tomatoes."

I chuckle.

"They can't use them all. Tomato plants are prolific. They shoot up and grow all over the place. They're thinking 'We've grown far too many and have used all we can so let's bag them up for the neighbors.' I'm not saying they are not good people, but they were overrun with tomatoes, so they gave them away." And that is what we are trying to create in our hearts. We're trying to grow too much love. Because when we have that level of abundance, we have the ability to give extraordinarily, even profoundly. But when we are not feeling abundance, we are feeling scarcity, and then we have trouble giving anything, even things like time and attention. Abundance is the source of the giving. So how do we create abundance? Drumroll please . . . through gratitude. And so, in the end, when we drill down to the very bottom, in order to improve another human being's life, the first thing I need to do is get grateful about mine. And when I get grateful about my life, all these things line up so neatly. I go from gratitude to abundance; from abundance to being a good giver; from being a good giver to creating human value; and from creating human value to life improvement. It flows perfectly.

How we create gratitude in a meaningful and substantive way becomes the most important question in this entire process. People really don't understand how to mine for gratitude and it's not their fault. We have had very poor instruction on how to be grateful. When I ask most people 'What are you grateful for?', what do you think comes up? Their family? #1. Great. What else? Friends? Money? Assets? Faith, love, and so on. I get Maslow's hierarchy spelled out. However, most of the answers are so broad they carry no power at all. If I say I'm grateful for my family, what does that even mean? We must go deeper to find the real gratitude. Who in your family are you grateful for today? Why? What is it about them that makes you grateful? The purpose of gratitude mining is simply to move my heart. I'm trying to stimulate this machine in here (points to chest), and by stimulating this machine I am moving myself into a space of abundance, which is where all the other good things happen. It's just an exercise to move my frame. So, if I say family, I don't feel much. That doesn't do a whole lot. And if you do daily gratitude practices, you can't say family every day! It just doesn't work. Going deeper—really mining for gratitude—is the only way to make this practice meaningful and sustainable. Here are four easy ways to create meaningful and rich gratitude experiences every day. Here in Hawaii (where Eric currently resides), I call it the Mahalo mindset, which is the idea of being able to channel gratitude. I have a gratitude journal which I started in 2011 with three entries every day and no missed days through today. It was a discipline that I tried to see if I could execute. I have it in the notes on my phone so I have no excuses that my gratitude journal is not near me. I have ten years just played out every day, day by day. These four techniques are the ones that I have found to give me the best results. The first is

1) **Journalistic**. This is where we're setting the stage and looking at the who, where, why, and how, and most importantly *what I am feeling* about all these things. It's like setting the stage of a story. For example, yesterday at 3:00 p.m., I was walking outside. It's the earliest I've seen an owl come outside. Yes, we have owls in Hawaii! It soared straight over my head. It clearly had his eye on something yummy and was just chasing that thing down. He had gorgeous brown and golden feathers that spread out above me. The sun was shining, and the sky was blue. It was the most impressive thing. If I had jumped and reached my hand up, I would have missed him by maybe a few inches! That's how close he was, and I felt this power and energy and this surge of love for the land and for life and for animals and prey; the circle of life. It was just very full. That's journalistic gratitude.

2) **Sensory**. This relies on physical or metaphysical senses. What did I see, hear, feel, taste, and smell? What spiritual movement happened for me during this experience? It doesn't even have to be event-driven—it can be contemplatively driven. I might be thinking about a concept, but I have these sensory experiences around this concept. Sometimes gratitude gets stuck in the events of the day, which is still a great way to mine for gratitude, but it doesn't have to be about the events of the day. It can just be what's happening inside of you. I was just thinking about my recent travel from Pennsylvania to Hawaii and marveling at the fact that I was able to sit in a plane, a metal tube, and get jostled around and soar through the atmosphere and make a journey that took the original missionaries nine months to complete in the span of just twelve hours! I was able to do it in a single day! How did that make me feel spiritually? I was honed in on what an extraordinary benefit I have in this world.

3) **Meme style**. You can write your own Mahalo mindset style meme by starting with the words "that moment when." This is a really successful way to start gratitude mining. You have to finish the moment and then say "because" and then fill in the rest. The "because" is where all the good stuff comes out, so you need to really explore why this moment means something to you and write down what you discover. If you don't know your "because," you really miss out on the point of the gratitude. Here's an example: "That moment when I get back to my house after a long day at work and my sixteen-year-old daughter sees me pull up in the driveway and runs out the front door to greet me with her math test in hand and a smile so big it barely fits on her face, and I realize she's been waiting for me to get home she could share it with me in person. This is so fantastic for me because I realize that my girl wants me to be proud

of her, and she chose to share the celebration of something wonderful with me, and I feel like the most important human being in the world."

4) **"Otherish."** The opposite of being selfish is being "otherish." This gratitude exercise is where the gratitude is in fact a letter . . . a Mahalo letter to someone to whom I owe a thank you. It could be to someone I haven't seen since I was four years old, or it could be a thank you to someone from yesterday. Regardless, when I channel that person and thank them for what they've done for me and explain why it mattered, I can't help but have my heart moved with gratitude. When we say, "thank you," that is, in fact, what gratitude is—saying thank you. And when we channel that to another human being, it really becomes a remarkable and profound gratitude experience. Our heart moves from gratitude when we point our gratitude specifically and intentionally.

That's the point of these four methods . . . to create specificity and intention. It's really powerful, but the trick is recognizing that the smallest details—the specificity, that is—is where the greatest power lies. I like to say that gratitude is the same thing as atomic physics. All the power of the universe is in a proton and electron and the relationship between them. All the power of the universe! That's why a hydrogen bomb does what it does. The smaller and more granular I get in my gratitude mining, the more profound the gratitude is. If I want to get heart movement, I've got to get small. If I'm talking big, the heart won't move. It just won't. It's not enough. Here is an example of getting granular:

What are you grateful for? My family

In your family, who? In my family I'm grateful for my daughter. Ok, why? Because she is really special to me Why? [You just have to keep asking the questions until you get super small.]

Why? Ok, because my sixteen-year-old daughter still has four freckles left on her beautiful face, and when she was seven years old, she was covered in freckles . . . and when I see those four freckles, I'm just so grateful that I can still see that the seven-year-old is still alive in this sixteen-year-old body. And then . . . BOOM! The heart moves! It's just like nuclear physics.

The biggest problem with gratitude is an ugly word called *entitlement*, or what we believe we deserve. If you look hard enough at any human suffering (not physical suffering but emotional suffering), the source of the conflict that's causing the suffering is an issue of entitlement between two or more parties. Each party feels that they are entitled to something from the other that they are not receiving. Man against universe, or man against man. It's this sense of entitlement that causes all suffering. When we divorce ourselves from all entitlement—which is hard work—remarkable things happen. The hard truth is that we don't really deserve anything . . . we actually deserve nothing. This might sound like a dark perspective, but it's just the opposite. It's not "I don't deserve anything" (in a voice of self-pity) like that, it's more like "I don't deserve anything" (in a calm, confident, and measured voice). The universe just is. I don't deserve anything from it. I get to choose my actions. I get to choose my responses. I get to have dominion over how I interact in that space. Sometimes things will work out for me, sometimes they won't work out for me. Either way, I didn't deserve it, and I'm not entitled to anything.

But here's the important part. When I am unentitled and I believe I don't deserve anything, I have the ability to be grateful for *everything*! Gratitude is limited by our sense of entitlement. The more entitled we are, the less grateful we can be. The more entitlements

I crowd into my life, the fewer the spaces there are for gratitude. The simplest example: You're breathing air right now. Do you deserve it? It just is. Do you deserve to live? Sorry, you don't. This sounds awful, but it's actually the opposite. It's so beautiful because we can recognize that everything we are experiencing is a gift. The hard moments? They are gifts. The good moments? Yes, they're gifts, too. The sunshine? The rain? It's all a gift, and we can't get there if we are holding an entitlement about what we think we deserve. Because if we receive something that we think we deserve, our answer usually isn't "I'm so grateful that I received this," rather it's "damn right! Of course, I received that, because I deserve it!" And so, there is a limitation that gets created for being able to be truly grateful for something because we believe we are entitled to it. Stripping entitlements is a really big part of experiencing gratitude. I can say this after doing it for ten years. Sometimes I get stuck in my journaling of gratitude and can't seem to find anything to put in writing. And I think, "what is it that I'm not able to find gratitude for right now that I should be? Where are these things that I should be grateful for?" And sure enough, I'll find an entitlement that's limiting my ability to perceive gratitude.

I ask Eric a question: "What are the benefits you see from practicing gratitude on a regular basis?"

By actively journaling my gratitude every day, I am much more aware of the opportunities for gratitude. I know that tomorrow morning when I wake up, I'll have my phone open, and I'm going to need entries for my journal. Because I know that I'll need to have those entries tomorrow, I'm already looking for things to be grateful for today. While this is not true for every person, I think the majority of human lives have roughly the same amount of sadness, hardship, heartbreak, beauty, wonder, joy, and contemplation when viewed over a thirty-year span. And if we have roughly equal amounts of those experiences, then we can take this painting of our life, this abstract painting of all these different colors, the yellows and the oranges of joy and the blue that is sadness, the browns and grays that are depression, all these different colors in the painting of our lives that represent these different experiences we have. The question is not "What are the different colors on your canvas?" We all have the same colors on our canvas and probably in similar proportions to each other. The question is "What colors do you notice the most?" In my mind, we have two ways to enter each day. Am I focused on the dark colors and therefore seeing how even more dark colors can show up in my day today? Or am I looking at the bright colors and seeing all of those bloom throughout my waking hours? I'm not trying to deny emotional states.

It's important that we have a variety of emotional states for mental health, I get that. I'm talking about where we want to focus our attention. By practicing the discipline of journaling my gratitude, I have a voice constantly reminding me: "Don't forget to look for all the yellows and oranges today." It's like putting a frame around the canvas that really calls out the colors I want to see. Gratitude journaling as a practice puts a frame on things. When I put a yellow frame on that canvas, all the yellow jumps right out at me. If I put a brown frame on the canvas, brown is going to jump out for me. So, what is the frame I want to put on my day? When we journal and practice gratitude, we end up putting ourselves in a position where we frame our day for joy, happiness, and love. And that leads to lots of capacities, which, in turn, leads to abundance, which leads to being a good giver, which leads to creating human value, and that allows us to improve lives.

Are you beginning to see a connection here? What things today can you find to be grateful for? What color will your frame be tomorrow?

The fulcrum for this whole thing is in that gratitude moment. How does this affect my daily life? How does it show up in our business? By framing. Framing every interaction, every conversation with that mindset of "Oh, I'm supposed to be mining for gratitude in this moment." Oh, I had this uncomfortable conversation with an employee who's not doing well. I'm going to look for the moments that are enlightening; that are gratitude moments in this space and journal about it tomorrow. It changes the way I approach the conversation. It's no longer as full of vitriol and conflict, but rather I'm thinking about what I'm going to be grateful for in this conversation for tomorrow. It's a reframing of the entire experience.

> What recent conversation held this opportunity for you? How could you have approached it differently?

In my business, we employed what came to be known as 2:00 p.m. circles where people would have to leave whatever they were doing to come together in a quick gratitude round. It always had a profound impact. The stuff that they would yield would surprise me every time I was there; I was amazed at how beautifully they could mine for gratitude. They were so good they became gratitude ninjas! That was always such a joyful experience. Another practice that we had internally, when we were really at our best, is that we would not start any conversation in an office with another person without first asking what are you grateful for? And then asking for the question back. Every conversation started with gratitude; if someone comes into my office who is really worked up about something I say, "Ok, just grab a seat. I can see you're upset, but before we start, what are you grateful for today?" And oh my gosh the shift! It was visceral! Just to watch them go, whoa, whoa, wait, what? All the anger would just drain out. All the frustration would just drain out. And then they could get vulnerable, and we could solve problems.

I asked Eric about the benefits of creating a Life Improvement Business. What difference did it make?

Best ever would be the answer. Our culture got so strong and so specifically flavored that our culture became kind of an electromagnet. The right people were very attracted to us and wanted to work for us. And the wrong people were repelled. Hiring and retaining became much simpler. We had our lowest turnover ever from 2012 to about 2017, which was the height of our execution of this. I left for Hawaii in 2018. I'm going to own that a little bit and say I wasn't there to be the cheerleader that I was before. During those years, we were in the top 5 percent for turnover in the industry for salespeople. The average tenure for auto salespeople is nine months. We were doing really profound work on retention. The other benefit revealed itself in the ways new hires who were not the right people responded to our culture. Instead of it taking six months to two years to work their way out of the company, they were gone in three weeks. Effective salespeople who didn't match our cultural beliefs would say "You people are really nice. I can't work here." Yea, hurray! We love that. We would give them a really good send-off, too. We wouldn't say "get out of here." We got them a cake and said, "thank you for your contributions, we're so glad you were here, and stay in touch!" Profitability skyrocketed!

We had our most profitable years during that period, and it wasn't because we were chasing money, it was because we were chasing love, which is beautiful, ironic, and hilarious. Who would have guessed that? We just stopped chasing the money. I'm not saying we weren't still business oriented and didn't measure and do all the things that businesses need to do, it just wasn't first on the list anymore. Instead, our priorities were all about developing people and developing culture. In terms of our customers, we had an incredible upswing in customer retention both in the service and sales operations. The community support was really rewarding. Our people were bringing opportunities to serve the community to us because they felt all this abundance all this love. They were thinking "how do we do more of this?" "How do we broadcast this in a different way?" Community engagement, which was a passion for me, showed up in our people not because of me but because of what they were experiencing themselves.

The movement that they were experiencing in their hearts brought them to say, "I'm feeling all this abundance; I have all these tomatoes, and I want to give more. How can I do that?" Watching our people take their own time and putting it into community effort was truly rewarding. They were working Sundays for nonprofits and events and supporting in profoundly beautiful ways because they wanted to. And you know, car guys aren't like that. We really had something beautiful growing. A really fundamental piece of growing a culture like that is changing the nomenclature, and so we started to abandon traditional words and instead used words that aligned with this belief system. We didn't have car salespeople, we had life improvement specialists, and we genuinely believed that. And by the way, that was on everyone's card. Everyone's card read life improvement specialist because that was what we were there to do.

What does the title of *manager* mean in a Life Improvement Business? Not a whole lot. It was everyone's role to improve lives. A customer doesn't need to know the hierarchy in a company to understand what we're going to do for them. My card says I'm a life improvement specialist . . . so I'm going to improve your life. It doesn't matter if I'm the owner, a manager, someone who cleans cars, or processes paperwork . . . I'm going to improve your life. It was an interesting thing to see this transformation happen. Initially, there was some resistance to this change inside the company. But once the lightbulb triggered in enough people, it just overflowed. People started to realize that they all wanted to be life improvement specialists. Yes! Exactly! That's what you want to be! This stopped being about work, and it started being about joy. We were hardly perfect, but in our best days and moments, our people were doing this because they wanted to do it. It wasn't about the job, and it wasn't because my boss says, or I need this paycheck, it was about the joy that comes from loving other people. And finding fulfillment by serving others. When those moments happened, it was the most brilliant.

> And to think that it all starts with personal gratitude. That is the seed that germinates into this extraordinary vine and grows over everything.

Watching people who had been permanent frowners or the people who had been the naysayers or the people who had been difficult; just watching that transition as they softened and became life improvement specialists, was so extraordinary. I firmly believe that just about everybody really wants to do this—to improve lives by creating human value—deep down in their core. When I tell these stories, I get told "Impossible" all the time, and that's fair. If I told you with zero experience in building a spaceship in the year 1821 you should build a spaceship, you would tell me it's impossible. But if I walk you through each development and technology that made spacecraft possible, you would see it as possible. It just has to start at the very bottom, which is gratitude. Once the gratitude is in place, and once the ritual is there and the heart movement starts, the next step becomes possible. And then the next one becomes possible. And the next one . . . suddenly impossible is no longer impossible. It's just one granular piece at a time.

As a teacher you are in the business of love; the life improvement business. The more grateful and abundant you are, the more you have to give away and create value for your students.

*Gratitude is when memory is stored in the heart and not in the mind.*

Lionel Hampton

## MAKING IT REAL

Gratitude becomes possible when we make it practical. When we decide to act on gratefulness, it becomes real. At its core, like every other decision, it is a pain/pleasure issue. If we know we can live a more fulfilled and happy life through gratefulness, is the pleasure of not writing in a gratitude journal or not writing a thank you card or not writing a gratitude letter or not mining for gratefulness in your day greater than the pain of what you are missing out on? Gratitude letters have been shown to provide happiness to both the writer and the receiver. In fact, some research shows that the more letters that are written, the more happiness and less depression can be experienced.

Research shows that the benefits of joy and happiness from a gratitude letter accumulate over time. Writing a letter brings one level of joy and satisfaction. Mailing or delivering it to the individual you are writing to brings another. But delivering the letter in person and reading it to that individual takes this exercise to another level. I've become a habitual thank-you card writer over the years. My mother taught me that no deed should go unnoticed and should be rewarded with a thank-you card. My rule of thumb is that if something takes someone more than fifteen minutes to complete on my behalf, it deserves a thank-you note. I have been thanking people in a formal manner almost all my life, but I had never written a gratitude letter, much less delivered it in person and read it to that individual. If anyone was deserving of one it was, in fact, my mother. By the time I decided to actually write, deliver, and read the letter to my mom, she was living in a nursing home and nearing the end of her life. She had some cognitive impairment but not enough that she couldn't comprehend or appreciate this gesture I was going to be making. She was the kind of person who was always in her children's corner, even when we didn't deserve it. There was not one day in my life that I didn't feel loved as long as she was on this earth. She was a naturally grateful, loving person who would do anything for anyone. As she was coming toward the end of her life, I wanted her to know what she had done for mine. She deserved that. I wrote the letter and planned on delivering it the next day. As I entered her room, I became somewhat apprehensive. I knew I would not be able to make it through without becoming emotional, but I pressed on and began to read:

*Dear Mom,*

*This is a letter of thanks and love to one of the most amazing women I have ever known. You've taught me so much. Probably the most important is how to love because you showed it to me all the time. Even when I didn't deserve it, you were an example of love, compassion, and patience. You allowed me to grow and make mistakes in order to create my own life's path. There has not been one day of my life that I didn't feel loved and supported mostly because of you. I also watch and am in awe of your bravery. You have been in a wheelchair for more than twenty years, yet you don't complain, and you continue to try and improve the lives of those around you in any way you can. With half their body in paralysis, weaker people would have given up, but not you. Every time I see you, I can count on a smiling face and cheerful disposition.*

*Thank you also for being a loving and kind mother-in-law to my wife and grandmother to my children. Your example of kindness and joy is a gift to them. You have also given them the time and attention that you gave all your children with unwavering patience. My kids will enjoy enduring memories of their grandmother.*

*I also want to thank you for being an example of a powerful woman. It has led to an appreciation for the women in my life, including my sisters, wife, and daughter. Some of the best supervisors and bosses I've had have been women. I look to them as equals and appreciate their intelligence and wisdom. It was your example and teaching that showed me this path. As a female, you demanded a certain kind of treatment. Not because of your words, but because of your actions. What a gift to me. The women I've known in my life have given me great guidance, love, and friendship. I was able to receive that because of you.*

*Finally, I want you to know how much I love you. This letter is a gift to you but also to me. I know this experience will bring me joy, frankly, for many years to come. Thank you for loving me, guiding me, being consistent with me, teaching me, challenging me, and most of all for being my mother. I know how much you loved being a parent, and I wanted to let you know how much I loved being your son.*

*All my love,*
*Mike*

This was an experience I will treasure forever. The research tells me that she got as much joy from hearing this as I did from writing it. Being in the room with her confirmed this for me. I did not completely make it through the letter without getting emotional, but the joy it had given both my mom and me was a gift that I'll revel in for a lifetime.

## WHO DESERVES YOUR LETTER?

> Gratitude can transform common days into Thanksgivings, turn routine jobs into joy, and change ordinary opportunities into blessings.
>
> William Arthur Ward

 *HIGH-PERFORMANCE ACTION!*

What are you willing to commit to in your life to raise your level of living in a more grateful way; actions that will benefit both you and your students? The following are some ideas to consider:

1. A daily or weekly gratitude journal that can be written out by hand or done on your phone or computer

2. A daily or weekly thank-you card to a person who you are truly grateful to or for

3. A gratitude letter or series of letters over a period of time that's more in-depth and specific than a thank-you card

4. Mining for gratitude on a daily basis and looking for something to be grateful for in every situation you encounter

List your actions below:

........................................................................................................................

........................................................................................................................

........................................................................................................................

........................................................................................................................

........................................................................................................................

*As we express our gratitude, we must never forget that the highest appreciation is not to utter words, but to live by them.*

*John F. Kennedy*

## GRATEFULNESS IN THE CLASSROOM

In her TEDx Talk "How thanking awakens our thinking" University lecturer and gratitude researcher Dr. Kerry Howells (2013) says, "If we thank while we think, we think in a more awake and engaged way." She feels a critical question in all learning is "What stops us from being awake?" and feels gratitude is a profound way to be awake and engaged for learning. She believes that "the quality of learning and the quality of thinking that takes place is really dependent upon the inner attitude that we bring to the learning situation." Consider the following research points regarding gratitude and school-age students:

- One study (Froh & Bono, 2012) found that gratitude played a key role in positive mental health for teens. Those teens who were more grateful experienced fewer behavior issues at school and were less likely to abuse alcohol and drugs. The study was completed over four years. Increases in gratitude over that time period were strongly correlated to happiness, positive attitude, life satisfaction, and hope. The authors noted that gratitude may be significantly connected to critical skills such as cooperation, purpose, creativity, and persistence.

- Younger students (ages eight to eleven) who were exposed to a purposeful gratitude curriculum showed an increase in more grateful thinking and mood, greater recognition of the benefits of other's thoughtful actions toward them, and increases of grateful thinking and positive emotions over time (Campbell, 2017).

- Other research has shown that gratitude might play a protective role in the lives of at-risk youth (Ma et al., 2013).

Though more research needs to done, the benefits of gratitude in a school setting show great promise, especially as we recognize the importance of social and emotional learning. Here are some suggestions that might be helpful:

1. Gratitude Journaling: Once a week, have students write three things in a journal for which they are grateful. Help them to get granular and specific. The more in-depth the gratitude, the more heart movement can take place. The entries don't have to be long, maybe just a few sentences.

2. Gratitude Circles or Rounds: Make it physical! This can be considered a brain break or class cohesion activity. Have students stand in circles and toss a ball in a repeated pattern. Every time a student receives the ball, they should state something they are grateful for. The pattern can be changed or reversed, and groups can be switched.

3. Gratitude Charts: Put students in small groups to chart their objects of gratitude. These charts can be word oriented, picture oriented, or a combination of both.

4. Gratitude Mining: As students prepare for their weekly gratitude journal entries, teach them to mine, notice, or look for things throughout the week they can include in their entries. This will heighten their experience in noticing new things around them for which to be grateful.

5. Gratitude Letters: As a class or as individuals, have students write a letter of gratitude to someone in the school for whom they are grateful and explain why. Have them be specific as possible. If possible, have students deliver and read the letter to the intended person.

Maybe the most important thing for students is that you practice gratefulness as a regular experience and share those experiences with your students. Being a role model in this area will have a great influence on their own practice.

#  REFLECTION

How can you be more of a role model for your students regarding becoming a more grateful person? What can you do to create a more grateful classroom?

Write your response here:

.................................................................................................................

.................................................................................................................

.................................................................................................................

.................................................................................................................

.................................................................................................................

.................................................................................................................

.................................................................................................................

# ONE MORE GRATITUDE QUOTE FOR THE TEACHER LOUNGE

*Gratitude is riches. Complaint is poverty.*

Doris Day

# HABIT #5

················································

## MAKE THE MORNING COUNT

YOU KNOW THAT FEELING WHEN YOU WAKE UP IN
THE MORNING AND YOU'RE EXCITED FOR THE DAY?
THAT'S ONE OF MY MAIN GOALS IN LIFE.

KIRSTEN DUNST

 IN THIS CHAPTER YOU'LL READ ABOUT

- The power of a morning routine
- The morning routines of real teachers
- My morning routine and its importance in beginning the day

Benjamin Franklin wrote that "Early to bed, early to rise, makes a man healthy, wealthy and wise." I'm not going to suggest what time you should call it a night but rather recommend you take full advantage of an early rise. Mark Twain did actually suggest what exactly to do with your morning time:

*Eat a live frog first thing in the morning and nothing worse will happen to you the rest of the day.*

What a perspective! I'm also not going to suggest you eat a live frog each morning. The problem for teachers is that Twain's quote might not be true. The most difficult tasks of a teacher's day almost never happen in the early morning. Rather, they happen during the school day. Mornings that excite, energize, and motivate create a mindset that allows you to take on those difficulties with better perspective and more energy. Research shows that coming to work in a bad mood can negatively impact your work (Rothbard & Wilk, 2011). Mood affects performance. Conversely, being in a good mood is correlated with an improved quality of work. Creating and practicing a daily morning routine can ensure the best possible mood in which to greet your students. Want to prepare yourself for the rest of the day, lower stress levels, boost energy, and increase productivity? Look no further than the creation of a morning routine.

Understanding the "why" of a morning routine is critical. If you don't, a powerful personal connection might not be established, and the motivation to put time and energy into a morning routine can fade. My "why" is knowing that a great start to the day is essential for living my life at the level to which I aspire. I connect it to my goals and dreams through feeling well and motivated first thing in the morning. Successful mornings take focus, planning, and repetition. Your students are depending on you to make your mornings count so you are at your very best. Triumphant mornings hold the possibility of creating peak physical and cognitive performance.

## THE MORNING ROUTINES OF REAL TEACHERS

The Internet had no shortage of fantastic morning routines of the most rich, famous, and successful people. From ice baths to cryogenic chambers to full tennis matches, these routines are fun to read about but, in many cases, are not practical for working teachers. What I've done is to ask real teachers to share their morning routines with you. Interestingly, I didn't ask these particular educators to participate because I knew they had a morning routine. I asked them because of how I perceived the quality of their professional lives and figured they must have a morning routine. In almost every case, I was right. Included in this list are entrepreneurs, bloggers, podcasters, administrators, and professional developers who are all practicing educators. Did their personalities produce the extraordinary results of their lives, or did their habits, such as a morning routine, establish and support their desire for excellence? By including their morning routines here, it makes it real, and the possibility of a morning routine becoming established in your life all the more likely. As I've stated elsewhere in this book, I provide these examples to offer what's possible, never to discourage.

Tracie Gunnufson is a third-grade teacher at Letford Elementary School in Johnstown, Colorado who has been in the field of education for seventeen years.

*Like so many other educators, I have seen a significant shift in education during my career. No doubt it has always been a very challenging and demanding job, but the past several years seem to have brought on a multitude of new challenges and expectations. An early-morning workout has made an immeasurable difference in navigating these ongoing challenges.*

*For the most part, I have always been a very active individual, but having recently started a new family and trying to balance the day-to-day of being a good mom with being a good teacher, it has seemed to have gotten the best of me. When it comes to time management, it was always exercise that was cut out. Combine that with a lack of sleep, and it spells trouble! What a huge mistake! While being cognizant of my health has always been important to me, I was failing to listen to my body even though I have an acute awareness of how critical it is to stay active, eat well, and get adequate sleep. I found myself tired all the time and beginning to notice aches and pains that I dismissed as "growing older."*

*Thankfully, I started playing a role in our district wellness program and was reminded of my passion for health and wellness. It was also a great reminder of the importance of self-care. After all, if I didn't take care of myself, how could I expect to take care of others in my quest to be a good mother, educator, and advocate for wellness? Before long, I took on a greater role in our wellness program, and I made it a point to get back on track and begin thinking about my own health. I was determined to get active again, not just in the summers when I had more time, but on a regular basis. This is what eventually led to a more regular routine each morning.*

*At first it sounded crazy to wake at 4:45 a.m. to work out before going to school! I told myself, "You already get up at 5:15 a.m. in an attempt to try to keep your head above water, which is already stretching it, what are you thinking?!" I wondered if I would be able to sustain this routine. It didn't take long, however, to begin seeing a change in my day. I saw a rise in my energy and motivation, more clarity in my thinking, less irritability with my family after a long day at work, subsiding aches and pains, and I was physically looking and feeling stronger.*

*Then, COVID-19 happened. The time and energy that consumed my days of teaching and navigating this new "normal" were insurmountable. Letting go of those 4:45 a.m. wake-up calls seemed to be the likeliest answer to add an extra layer of energy or a little more sleep, record a new video lesson, or have time to answer parent emails. But I can now say, without a doubt, that if it hadn't been for those 4:45 a.m. workouts, I absolutely know I would not have gotten through the craziest year of teaching yet. I truly believe my morning routine made it possible* to sustain the energy needed to conquer the 2020-2021 school year. Even now, during the summer when I'm free to slow down, sleep in a bit, and take on a slower pace, my husband thinks I'm crazy to still take on my 4:45 a.m. workouts. I do it because I know I will continue to have similar results. It has now become a nonnegotiable habit that will continue to make an appearance in my daily routine. What's more, I'm beginning to see this simple routine transform into a greater wellness program that I have no doubt will evolve into more purposeful action and add an extra layer of overall happiness and wellness. Today, I'm healthier and happier because of my morning routine.

> Morning is an important time of day, because how you spend your morning can often tell you what kind of day you are going to have.
>
> Lemony Snicket

## DAVID GUSITSCH

**David Gusitsch is a father of three and the principal of Saxe Middle School in New Canaan, CT. He loves learning and believes in educating the whole child. He also believes that relationships matter and that "kids don't care how much you know, until they know how much you care."**

The first thing I do in the morning is drink a full pint of water and then make the bed, even if it is just "my side" if my wife is still sleeping or our little guy has snuck into bed with us. I then proceed to do two sets of fifty push-ups and/or a morning exercise session. This varies depending on time of year and the "goings on" in life at any particular moment. Over the years, it has been a rotation of running, swimming, circuit training, or weight lifting, which typically lasts thirty to sixty minutes. This has been a routine since college. Morning swim practices are dreadful when going through them but apparently set you up for a lifetime of good habits and routines. Just like making the bed and drinking the water, the push-ups are a nonnegotiable habit that allows me to feel that I have at least accomplished a few things that are healthy and have started my day in the right way. Making the bed has been a commitment since first seeing the "University of Texas at Austin 2014 Commencement Address—Admiral William H. McRaven Make Your Bed" speech (the book is also great).

Finally, I shower, dress, and say goodbye to each family member (including the dog). My thirty-five-minute drive to school typically includes a podcast and a cup of coffee. Upon arriving at work, I read a quote from my daily calendar and map out the day. This always includes moments of gratitude to maintain perspective and begin the day with a positive mindset. Each day is an opportunity, and we get to choose the lens through which we view it. From here, I walk the building on my way to morning arrival where parents drop their children off for school. At arrival, Pandora plays upbeat music, and I greet each student who enters the building with a smile and a "good morning; nice to see you" or "have a great day." My goal is for every student to be acknowledged and know that they are seen, every day. This is a reciprocal practice as it fills my bucket to spread some positivity as well!

*I get up every morning and it's going to be a great day. You never know when it's going to be over, so I refuse to have a bad day.*

Paul Henderson

## JENNIFER CAPUTO

**Jennifer Caputo is a fifth-grade teacher who was the 2020 Sussex County Teacher of the Year and a New Jersey State Teacher of the Year finalist. She is a professional developer, graduate course instructor, and graduate course designer. She has developed a reputation of excellence for her expertise in the areas of mindfulness, mindful meditation, breathwork, and yoga. Jennifer is a wellness coach and healing facilitator and hosts the *Shift for Wellness* podcast. Visit Jennifer's Teachers Pay Teachers store and website: *Calm and Cool School* and get access to downloadable meditation, breathwork, and tapping mp3s and scripts for your classroom use.**

*Preparing for my day begins the night before. Scheduling a bedtime is paramount, and shutting off devices an hour before bedtime is a must. Powering down gives my brain the time it needs, and deserves, to settle down and prepare for a solid eight hours. The sleep routine begins when I walk in the door from school.*

*Avoiding alcohol after school is another practice. Alcohol interrupts my sleep, and I honor my sleep too much to allow that to happen. I replace alcohol with Sleepy Time tea or anything herbal and calming. Everything from the moment I walk through that door is an intentional preparation for slipping into sleep as effortlessly as possible, which means I bathe in the evening as well. A bath or shower at night helps to symbolically wash away the day and calm the nervous system. Then it's three notations in my gratitude journal and seven more said in my head as I get myself comfortable under the covers preparing for my beauty sleep!*

*All of these routines are in place because my morning routine is critical to the unfolding of each day. I wake to a natural alarm clock, which mimics a natural sunrise and gradually brightens to help me wake naturally. It's then set to birds chirping or chimes, about fifteen minutes later. Beginning my day with a jarring alarm is not an option.*

*Automatically, the prayers begin as I run through my stretching sequence before my feet even hit the floor. The sequence is not long, and it moves my spine in all six ways, activates my abdominal muscles, and gets my blood pumping. Once my feet land, getting the bed made is the first order of business. Then before the final pillow is set, I throw it on the floor and settle into morning meditation. I have no set type of meditation that I practice each morning. This time is very intuitive, and I go with whatever my body, mind, and spirit are asking for. I also don't have a set amount of time for meditation. It could be three, five, ten minutes, or more. I just go with it, and however long it is, is however long it needs to be.*

*Caffeine is also not a part of my diet, so I begin each morning with a tall glass of warm lemon water. Fifteen minutes later, I drink another tall glass of warm water with*

Ashwagandha, an adaptive herb that helps to calm the body, ease inflammation, and boost nutrition. Fifteen minutes after that, I eat my gluten-free/dairy-free breakfast that changes seasonally. Currently, it's blueberry chia seed pudding with honey and ginger. And yes, it holds me over until lunch!! Choosing a gluten-free diet because of a sensitivity has made a huge transformation in lessening the inflammation in my body and eliminating brain fog. It helps me to feel alive again.

Supplements are also very important to my morning routine. I don't take a multivitamin. Instead, I've had my general practitioner take blood work, and I've used the results to determine which supplements my body needs.

Finally, before I walk out the door, I lay down to do my seven-minute healing breathwork meditation, and that is what seals the deal for the day! The world could literally fall apart around me, as it had during COVID-19, and I can withstand it. Please give this meditation a try at shiftforwellness.com/ services/. It's an active breathwork meditation technique with a three-part breath done through an open mouth. It's very transformational and facilitates great release. At Shift, you will find a video tutorial, where I guide you through the meditation.

It's important to note that I use Sunday to prep for the week in terms of outfits and lunches, so that saves a lot of time in the morning. I choose five outfits that I think I'd like to wear and iron them all if needed. I select the jewelry and shoes and hang them in a certain section of the closet so I don't have to think about what I'm wearing when I get up in the morning. This is the perfect time to listen to my audiobook! In the past, thinking about what to wear used to make me not want to get out of bed. This is how I beat that mindset! Additionally, I'll bag salad lunches in advance so they're all set to pop into my lunch bag each morning, or I'll make a warm dish on Sunday that I can separate into five glass containers to grab and go! All quick. All healthy.

There's one more thing to add. During the breakfast routine, I boil water to fill two thermoses that I'm sure to drink throughout the day. Bringing an actual glass from the cabinet adds to the experience. I don't enjoy drinking out of a thermos or a bottle of water, nor do I want to contribute to the plastic dilemma.

If you're saying, "She's nuts! She's got nothing but time on her hands!" you'd be very mistaken. This routine is something that started small and increased over time. It wasn't easy for me at first, and sometimes it can still be a challenge, but I don't even think about these things anymore. They're a natural part of my day. They've been integrated into my morning and evening routine. I can be out of the house in an hour with all of these things in place, but I prefer not to rush, and I give myself an hour and a half. I could also be out of the house in ten minutes, but I know I'll only suffer as a result. I've been there, and it's not a happy place. It's a practice, a lifestyle, and it's what I choose to do each day in order to live my very best life and show up for myself in the best way I know how. For me, it's imperative to be my absolute best each day for myself first, and then for my family, friends, and students. I do all this to quiet my mind, heal my body, and nourish my soul.

The result is that I get what I intended: a quiet mind, a healthy body, and a nourished soul. In turn, this brings others into my world who are also calm, healthy, and nourishing. It also will bring in others in need of calm, healing, and nourishment, which allows me the opportunity and blessing to be able to work with them and teach them how to heal themselves. The energy that I create for myself each day directly transfers over to my students. If I'm grounded, they're grounded. I've been on this path since 2007, purposefully and intentionally working on it, after a journey through cancer.

Some people dream of success, while other people get up every morning and make it happen.

Wayne Huizenga

## DR. MISSY WIDMANN

**Dr. Missy Widmann is a health and fitness educator at Challenger Alternative High School in Spanaway, WA. In 2016, she was frustrated with punitive practices in schools as well as the devaluing of health and fitness programming in PreK–12 education. She partnered with a cognitive learning scientist, and they cofounded the nonprofit Neural Education (neuraleducation.org). The vision of Neural Education is to bring safety, structure, and a sense of belonging to every student and classroom by uniting the neuroscience of learning with the power of teaching.**

I am considered the "pumpkin" amongst my friends. Especially those who I have known as early as elementary school. My internal clock remains constant. Once 8:30 p.m. rolls around, I begin to shut down. My nightly shutdown is not the "sit in front of the TV" type of shutdown—where you still have enough energy to "zone out." This is a complete low battery shutdown.

With the nightly shutdown also comes the morning routine. I rarely sleep in. A late night does not ensure a later wake time. My sleep/wake cycle works hard to maintain consistency. Therefore, I unapologetically listen to my body and follow my natural circadian rhythms. The benefit of this routine is that a good night's sleep prepares the brain and body for a productive day.

Every day starts the same way—a cup of hot tea, a Kind Bar, and a workout. There is plenty of neuroscience research that supports the brain and body benefits of consistent workouts. For me, the most important positive outcome of the daily workout is the "gym thoughts." All of my best ideas start as a gym thought. My brain is awake, blood is pumping through my veins, and solutions to the previous day's problems become clear. This is also the time when I process the needs of my students, the deep "why" of the day's lesson. It is also where I create kinesthetic cognitive rehearsal activities for my students. There is nothing more effective when creating kinesthetic activities than being kinesthetic while creating them.

Sleep and gym thoughts have become so essential for my work that I will go to bed and tell myself, "The answer to (add issue or problem here) will come in the morning." This is a simple strategy that I learned from Dr. Kieran O'Mahony (my partner at Neural Education). Last year, during the COVID-19 education shifts, my sleep and workout routine became a mental health pillar. Educators were forced to become virtual educators overnight. It was a very stressful shift that required high levels of adaptability and technology knowledge. The learning curve was absolutely vertical! It was important to maintain a brain-aligned classroom in the virtual setting. Sleep and workouts became even more foundational as I led a team of Neural Educators as we cocreated brain-aligned, kinesthetic, virtual classrooms.

> When you arise in the morning, think of what a precious privilege it is to be alive, to breathe, to think, to enjoy, to love.
>
> Marcus Aurelius

## ANDY VASILY

**Andy Vasily is a pedagogical coordinator at The Kaust School in Saudi Arabia, workshop leader, educational consultant, and podcaster who considers himself to be a lifelong learner who is deeply committed to better understanding the guiding principles that help people to achieve their best and meet the goals they have set for themselves.**

As I venture down my own path of learning, what I have come to understand the most is that having solid routines and structures in place definitely helps me to live more purposefully and have a deeper sense of fulfillment and meaning in my life. Performing at my best both personally and professionally has required me to get super specific with strategies that work for me in my own context.

I'd like to take this opportunity to share some of these strategies and routines with hopes that you might have a gem or two to take away and apply in your own life. I'll use the acronym JEMR to categorize the different areas that are built into my regular morning routines and also how these routines spill over into other parts of my day. So, here we go. . . .

JEMR stands for journaling, exercise, meditation, and reading. Here is a bit about each of these areas:

(J) Journaling: I start off every morning with ten to fifteen minutes of uninterrupted journaling. I like to stack this habit on top of something else that I regularly do each day, which is to make a morning cup of coffee for my wife and me. While I am waiting for the coffee to brew, I simply write away in my journal about whatever is hot on my mind. It can be whatever I'm thinking or feeling in the moment, what I am reflecting on from the previous day, questions I am pondering, or my biggest hope for the upcoming day. The point is that journaling to me is an important habit to get my creative juices flowing and be able to record my ideas with regularity.

(E) Exercise: For me morning exercise is a must-do on my daily list. Whether it be a morning run (usually three to five miles), a workout at the gym, a long walk, or some light stretching, exercise lights me up in special ways. It allows me to feel the glow of endorphins running through my body and puts me into a more positive mindset to begin each day. It's always been a must-do for me and will continue to be for years to come.

(M) Mindfulness: Embedded within my mindfulness practice is meditation. I try, as much as possible, to meditate for ten to fifteen minutes each morning.

*If I miss my morning meditation, I try to get it done in the evening before bed. Mindfulness to me is just sitting with my breath and thoughts without judgment. I do not stick to any one style of meditation and give myself permission to create different versions of meditation that I can apply. Whether it be gratitude, visualization, sending compassion to loved ones and friends through my thoughts, or being as still and quiet as possible, meditation is a huge part of my mindfulness practice. Learning to sit with difficult emotions and thoughts is a critical part of this process. Rather than push away these emotions and thoughts, I try to invite them in and welcome them without judgment. Although there are times when I lose consistency with this practice, it is something I always return to and practice whenever I can. It has made a profound difference in my life.*

*(R) Reading: This is a special one that I've prioritized over the past year. I do have a very specific structure that I apply when it comes to my reading practice. I'm very deliberate with it and try to get it done both in the morning and at night. I will now explain how this works.*

*I have an account set up with Audible. I have certain books set up for me to listen to, but I also have a hard copy of each of these books. Audible has a speed setting that allows listeners to speed up the audio. What I do is set the audio to 1.3 or 1.4 times the regular speed. As I listen to the book being read at a much faster than normal pace, I am also following along in the hard copy of the book. This is great for the eyes as it requires me to follow along in the book and quickly scan each line on each page. The pace at which I follow allows me to develop the skill of speed reading, while still being able to take in all the words, ideas, and storylines being shared in the book. As I follow along while listening to the audiobook, I also highlight different things that stand out to me; for example, new vocabulary, concepts, names of researchers, quotes, and so on.*

*Once I have finished reading the book, I record notes on a Google Doc to keep track of my learning. Listening to the audiobook at 1.3 or 1.4 times the normal speed allows me to get through a book in about a week or so. Each morning, I try to get one chapter in or finish a chapter from the night before. This reading routine has been a game changer for me and has helped me to learn so much more over the past year. I highly recommend you give this a go. Tinker away with the speed settings to get it just right for you.*

*The routines I've described above have been modified and tweaked over the years. At times, I've let some of these habits and routines fall to the wayside, but I always find myself returning to them and building them back into my life with consistency. The most important thing is that through it all, I've developed a strong sense of routine in my life that has served me well. I continue to refine and explore what's possible with regard to important routines and give myself the flexibility to change things up when needed in order to be more efficient with my time and energy. I hope the things I've shared help to give you some new ideas to apply in your own life.*

Now that your eyes are open, make the sun jealous with your burning passion to start the day. Make the sun jealous or stay in bed.

Malak El Halabi

Matt Bergman is a former teacher turned digital learning specialist at a
K–12 private school. He is also a consultant, keynote speaker, blogger,
and podcaster. A self-described universal design for learning evangelist,
you can read his blog at bergman-udl.blogspot.com.

*I like to think of my morning routine as the primer for the rest of my day. Without
it, I am often lost and off kilter. Believe it or not, my morning routine begins the
day before when I write out my "Daily 7." My Daily 7 consists of the seven tasks
that I would like to accomplish the next day. Having something in writing helps
me stay focused even through distractions that are bound to happen.*

*I begin the day with a five-minute visualization meditation. I close my eyes and
focus on my breathing. With each inhale, I silently repeat a mantra that I have
developed over time and mentally envision myself going through it. The mantra
is the following:*

*Relax*

*Listen*

*Surrender judgment and ego*

*Love, joy, peace, patience, kindness, gentleness, and self-control*

*Be strong and courageous*

*Be water*

*I use this mantra as a way to remember the values that I want to live by and shape
my interactions with others. Although I am not perfect, it helps a great deal. After
my meditation, I usually begin with reading. I set a timer and read five minutes from
the Bible.*

*Next, I embark on a quick five-minute prayer exercise. I have a prayer journal
where I have written out passages from the Bible that deal with various things I
might be going through such as anger, frustration, joy, or happiness. I read that
scripture verse and use it to pray for something going on in my life. I then pick a
particular person that I feel I need to pray for such as someone I am struggling
with or someone who needs help.*

*I then do a five-minute affirmation exercise. I love Norman Vincent Peale and
his 40 Thought Conditioners. I will pick a thought conditioner and handwrite it
five times. Writing it out helps it stick within my subconscious for the remainder
of the day.*

*I then read a personal development book for fifteen minutes. I set a timer so that
I don't go over my limit. Lately, I have been reading about how to improve my
listening and people skills.*

*Finally, I set a timer for –five to ten minutes and go on Twitter. I look for new ideas in educational technology that I could use, share, or infuse into learning.*

*I do all of this because I have found that I need to create a strong mental foundation to begin the day. When I was in high school and college, I learned the importance of visualization and performance as a football player. It was a great way to stay focused as you took the hits, twists, and turns from the game. We learned that a game never goes as expected—neither does life.*

*I recently rekindled this practice over the past two years. I was frustrated by my inability to deal with the twists, turns, and frustrating moments throughout the day. I began using this routine as a way to prepare for the "hits" that would come my way. By preparing and priming my mind for the challenges, tasks, and successes of the day, I have found myself benefiting in many ways. First, I am not as stressed, rather I am focused. When distractions come my way, I can easily adapt and then refocus. I am more present with the people in my life. When challenging situations arise, I remember the values that I want to embody. I'm also more efficient. Having a list of tasks made the day before is helpful, especially when distractions pop up.*

Do not shorten the morning by getting up late; look upon it as the quintessence of life, as to a certain extent sacred.

Arthur Schopenhauser

## CHRIS WALKER

**Chris Walker has been an elementary physical educator for twenty-four years at the same school, Hillsborough Elementary in North Carolina. He is also the NCSHAPE president and has served in the state organization for more than seven years. He is also a national/international presenter to physical educators and health and classroom teachers.**

*I work out to push myself in terms of fitness. The reason I do so is to be in a better physical and mental state to teach my students each and every day. Each week I continue to try new fitness activities and workout sessions that are challenging to me because I ask my students to try new and challenging things in my class. If I ask them to try it, I demand it of myself.*

*I have been working out with the schedule listed below for a bit over two years. Prior to that, I had been teaching and working out Monday, Wednesday, and Friday for thirteen years.*

*Here is how I prepare myself each day physically. This routine also helps me get mentally stronger because I push myself each workout. If I have a not-so-great exercise session, I reassess what led to that and plan accordingly to be more successful when I am training myself the next day. I would do the same if my lesson is not solid or if my students are not able to grasp a concept that I am teaching. I rethink, reassess my approach, and change it to try and deliver a better lesson to the class I'm teaching.*

*My morning routine is that of movement and lots of it. Monday through Friday I rise a bit after 4:00 a.m. each day. Saturday and Sunday, I tend to wake around 6:00 a.m.*

*On Monday, Wednesday, and Friday, I head to an outdoor location to lead a bootcamp style class from 5:00 a.m. to 5:45 a.m. From there, I journey to a local gym and begin my own workout that starts around 6:05 a.m. At 7:00 a.m., my next client arrives, and I train him for forty-five minutes. I then head home to shower and shave before I arrive at school to start my day with students.*

*On Tuesday and Thursday, I leave my home at 4:15 am to a nearby town to teach my crossfit-ish class that has my own unique spin to it. My classes begin at 5:00 a.m. and 6:00 a.m. Some days, I train with my clients, and on other days, I arrive earlier to get in a workout. After training and cleaning up, I am back at home to get ready for school.*

*Saturdays and Sundays are my high cardio days in addition to working out. I either work out first and then play soccer for a couple of hours, or I go for a three- to six-mile run. There have been times that I may ride an indoor cycle or elliptical for an hour. It just depends on how much I want to push myself.*

*This is me in a nutshell. Each night, I give thanks for a great day and do meditative breathing to relax before hitting repeat.*

An early-morning walk is a blessing for the whole day.

Henry David Thoreau

## MY MORNING ROUTINE

I credit my morning routine with the excitement and joy to greet each day. It provides me with the mental nourishment and motivation to start the day, take on the challenges that lie ahead, and enjoy the successes should they come to pass. By the time I finish, I feel great! I've already created momentum to have a great day, and that's what I'm after. A morning routine can set the tone for the entire day. I look forward to it each day and the ensuing "lift" it provides. Believe me, I notice when I don't do it, which happens less than five times a year. It's very precise and looks like this:

- Like some of the morning routines you've already read about, mine starts the night before. I don't do a lot, but I do check my schedule. I've never transitioned to a calendar, or note, or app. I keep a leather-bound calendar, which I have done for years, and a small book of notes, ideas, and to-do lists. I check them both before I go to bed, so I have peace of mind that I won't be forgetting anything first thing in the morning. It actually comforts me and allows me to relax.

- I rarely set an alarm unless I have a very early appointment or engagement. My body naturally wakes around 6:30 a.m., which works well for my schedule.

- Upon waking there are two main things I do, and the first is meditate. I've already written about meditation, so I don't need to do it again here, but it does clarify and energize. It's the best possible medicine I can give my brain first thing in the morning. When I'm done, I am ready to tackle the first part of my day but not yet . . .

- The second thing I do is a carefully created visualization where I am intentional about both goal setting, or what I want my life to look like, and being grateful. It's very precise though some of the details vary from day to day. I actually listen to specific music which I have set on YouTube. One composition is called "World's Most Inspiring & Uplifting Instrumental Music" by Gunta K. Freidenfelde and the other is called "Limitless–Powerful Motivational Music Mix" no composer given. During this time, I am both visualizing/creating the life I expect and giving thanks for the life I already have all at the same time. It took some time to get the process where I wanted it to be, but now I have been doing it for years. I divide it into four areas—(1) career, (2) financial considerations, (3) my physical body, and (4) relationships. It becomes an extremely motivating and carefully crafted movie in my head. When I finish, I am ready for the day with excitement and passion.

- Once I finish, the next significant thing I do is take care of my body nutritionally. I always keep a gallon of distilled water in the refrigerator. I mix in a greens product (with ingredients like wheat and oat grass) and baking soda in order to help alkalize my bloodstream. I then have oatmeal with almond milk, stevia, raisins, and banana.

- Sometimes I exercise when my schedule allows but not usually. I get my physical work done either over lunch or after work. So, while I highly recommend exercising in the morning because of all the benefits, I normally don't do it at that time.

- Finally, I make my bed. I'm now ready to start the day and head into the office.

- It bears mentioning that at one time I used Tony Robbin's Priming Exercise in the morning. I experienced it live with Tony in 2014, and it got my attention. I enjoyed it especially with thousands of other people doing it at the same time. It has physical, breathing, and visualization/spiritual/gratefulness aspects to it. It does prime your brain for action. It helped me to develop the visualization practice I use today. I strongly suggest you give it a try. You might want to add it to your morning routine as well. It only takes about fifteen minutes, and it can put you in a very productive mindset. You can find it by going to YouTube and searching for Tony Robbin's Priming Exercise.

You've now been exposed to the morning routines of real teachers who know to prioritize them in order to be at their very best by the time they get to school. It's a wonderfully selfish act that benefits everyone you come into contact with on any given day. It's a complete win/win for all involved. If you want to be at your very best each day for yourself and your students, I suggest you take a good look at what you do in the morning to ready yourself for the day ahead. Start with choosing one thing to practice in the morning. It might be something that makes you happy, content, or excited. Or, maybe it is something that makes you determined, forceful, and confident. It could include reading, practicing gratitude, exercising, meditating, visualizing, deep breathing, writing, journaling, or simply making your bed. The key is to make a decision in this moment and begin!

Doubt increases with inaction.

Clarity reveals itself in momentum.

Growth comes from progress.

For all these reasons, BEGIN.

Brendon Burchard

# REFLECTION

You've now had the opportunity to read through a number of morning routines full of variety and possibility. What are you considering establishing, changing, or adding to your morning routine?

Write your response here:

.................................................................................................................................................

.................................................................................................................................................

.................................................................................................................................................

.................................................................................................................................................

.................................................................................................................................................

.................................................................................................................................................

.................................................................................................................................................

.................................................................................................................................................

.................................................................................................................................................

.................................................................................................................................................

.................................................................................................................................................

.................................................................................................................................................

.................................................................................................................................................

.................................................................................................................................................

.................................................................................................................................................

.................................................................................................................................................

.................................................................................................................................................

.................................................................................................................................................

.................................................................................................................................................

.................................................................................................................................................

.................................................................................................................................................

.................................................................................................................................................

.................................................................................................................................................

.................................................................................................................................................

.................................................................................................................................................

.................................................................................................................................................

# PUTTING IT ALL TOGETHER

ADJUSTING TO A NEW PATH AND A NEW DIRECTION WILL REQUIRE NEW QUALITIES AND STRENGTHS, AND THESE QUALITIES ARE ALWAYS EXACTLY WHAT WE NEED TO ACQUIRE IN ORDER TO ACCOMPLISH THE GREAT THINGS AHEAD IN OUR LIFE.

RHONDA BYRNE

 IN THIS CHAPTER, YOU'LL READ ABOUT "SUCCESS"

- See the truth in order to identify your current habits and attitudes
- Understand the power of the moment in your ability to decide and move forward
- Create a plan to move forward in the most direct way possible
- Change your limiting beliefs to view risk as a realm of possibility versus limitation
- Enjoy the process to find satisfaction in both successful and challenging moments
- Start now! There is no time like the present to start designing the coming years of your life
- Surround yourself with success! Who you keep in your company matters.

I cannot stress enough that this book represents no judgment of, or expectations for, your life. The examples throughout the book are about what's possible and are meant to inspire, not discourage. Everyone is where they are. We all have unique starting points and stories. What we all have in common is hope and the ability to decide and move forward. I'm guessing that if you're reading this book, you're already doing at least something that I've prescribed. Whether you are or aren't doesn't matter. Choose one of the five habits that holds interest for you, or choose the one that is most accessible. Teachers lead extremely busy lives, and creating a new habit might be most attainable if you perceive it to be the most reasonable. Maybe that means beginning to walk, starting a gratitude journal, or changing your morning routine. Take the first step! Use the power of the moment and decide now. Then create a goal and action plan around it. Make it a short goal and action plan for only the first week. You'll see that it's attained, or you might have to adjust your plan, but either process will create momentum, movement, and energy. For example:

Goal

> I will make one entry into a gratitude journal every day for one week.

Action Plan

1. Download a note or gratitude journal app on my phone
2. Create a general list of things I'm grateful for
3. Make the entry in the same general timeframe each day
4. Mine for things to be grateful for every day in order to prepare for the next day's entry
5. Check my progress at the end of Week 1
6. Adjust goal for Week 2 or continue as planned

Why?

> Because I know I can create positive emotions in my life through daily gratitude. This will spill over into other parts of my life in order to bring a greater level of satisfaction and joy.

Resource Individual

> Eric Savage

Immediate Action

> Download my chosen app!

Next, the possibilities are endless. Maybe you create new goals around this same habit or maybe you add a goal around a second habit. Maybe you decide to focus on just one habit for a month, six months, or even an entire year. Or, maybe you add a goal around a new habit each week until you've created momentum around all five habits in the first five weeks. It's going to depend on your personality, willingness to commit, and the time you have for it. The point is to get a little better each day by making small, incremental progress.

I tend to jump in with both feet and watch what happens. I often choose to create change in many areas of my life all at once. Crazy change occurs when I have been most disciplined. In fact, I have a mantra I often use on myself. When I have a choice to make, I say to myself, "Mike, don't be lazy." A bit critical, but it works for me most of the time. When I started the process of writing this book, I upped my game in other areas of my life because I knew it would make for a better outcome for this project. I made sure I ate well, exercised every day, managed my stress through meditation, and practiced gratitude through my daily morning routine. Discipline can be inspiring. That discipline you have during the school year? Where you have to be in front of your students for an entire day and tend to countless things during that same time period? Channel that energy, and use it to your advantage now. The good news is that the hard thing becomes easier. What seems like a mountain top will become a small hill. Your mental muscles will become stronger, and you can keep reaching for new goals and new heights. The process of writing this book, though time-consuming, is much easier than previously because it's my fourth book! Creating a new habit is just like building muscle: You make small gains each day, week, and month. This is not an overnight process but one of daily change in small increments adding up to a life of satisfaction and joy.

#  REFLECTION

How will you begin your journey to a more satisfying and productive life? What will you do to get the ball rolling and create momentum going forward? What is the first step you are willing to take?

Write your response here:

........................................................................................................................

........................................................................................................................

........................................................................................................................

To help inspire and motivate I'd like to offer some words of encouragement; a "pep" talk, if you will. I hope that some of these ideas will ring true. I offer these thoughts through my version (there are many) of a **SUCCESS** acronym:

### **See the truth**

### **Understand the power of the moment**

### **Create a plan**

### **Change your limiting beliefs**

### **Enjoy the process**

### **Start now**

### **Surround yourself with success**

### *See the Truth*

*The truth will set you free, but first it will make you miserable.*

*James A. Garfield*

The pleasure in writing this book is sharing the concepts and ideas that continue to push me forward. It is truly about designing a life versus making a living. In that, I try to maintain some semblance of balance in my daily journey. The habits I've prescribed in this book help me do that. We all have days, weeks, and if we're lucky, even months at a time of maintaining a good balance in our lives that allows us to feel secure, optimistic, and like we can handle most things that come our way. But there are times when life knocks us off our perch, and balance seems like the furthest thing from our reality. Think about a calm day in the middle of the summer when the pressures of teaching seem a million miles away. Now compare it to a normal school day in the middle of spring. Maybe you are administering state tests, trying to keep students engaged as the weather turns warmer and brighter, or dealing with the daily pressures of lesson planning and execution, classroom management issues, and numerous administrative duties. All are scenarios that represent states of mind and perspective.

It's normal to allow events to determine our level of satisfaction and happiness, but we should be striving, as best we can, to choose to enter each day with the perspective that we can determine how we feel about the day ahead. In other words, to borrow the emotions from that distant July day so they can be used freely in the middle of April. You have that personal power and ability to make every Monday feel like Friday at 5:00 p.m., or to make what might be viewed as a daily grind seem like the greatest day of your life. The inclusion of these habits can be the rock we depend on to help us live life at that level. The more routine these habits become, the more they can provide comfort in our daily living.

What we need to do is to carefully examine our current habits and attitudes and seek our own truth about where to begin. Some people will dive right in and try to improve in many areas, but some will prefer to start with one or two habits. This will take some self-reflection and truth-seeking. In your examination of these five habits, what really needs improvement immediately? What do you need to take on first that might have the most impact on your life? The lives of your students? It's the answers to these questions that will serve as your guide as you begin this journey.

> We first make our habits then our habits make us.
>
> John Dryden

When reflecting upon your truth, it's important to realize that you are in charge; that you are personally responsible for everything that goes on in your life. You are a creator. To finally come to terms with this idea was a real eye-opener for me. The sooner you come to terms with it, the sooner you can live the life of your dreams. Life doesn't happen to you; life happens *because* of you. Your thoughts, intentions, emotions, and creations drive you forward. Look around! Everything from the smallest item to the most complex machine started in someone's imagination, and that is the beginning of the creative process. In my view, no part of your life is the result of chance, luck, or wishful thinking; rather, it is the direct result of your thoughts, actions, and faith. It might be difficult because there is an element of the unknown in trusting that this is possible. As you move through transformation, you will learn to use this creative process, and also, and maybe more importantly, remember or recognize that you have used this very process thousands of times in your life.

You are in control. Many people give up this control because they believe that random things happen to them, whether they be happy or sad, and they go through their days allowing life to be dictated to them instead of realizing that they are dictating life. Happy, loving, and joyful circumstances do not result in happiness, love, and joy. Happiness, love, and joy result in happy, loving, and joyful circumstances. The sooner you realize that you have the power to control your day through your thoughts and emotions, the sooner you'll be able to drink the very best juice life has to offer, purposefully.

It is tempting to shrug off responsibility to an outside influence that you brought into your path in the first place. Resist blaming others and outside influences for your own unique circumstances. Every minute you wait on this adjustment you deprive yourself of the full knowledge of what it is to lead a truly happy life. I am reminded of a quote from Elaine St. James:

> But I do know that if I see my life as my responsibility, then I can make the changes necessary to create what I want and need to be happy . . . I've learned that if there's something in my life that doesn't work, and I'm waiting for someone else to fix it, I'd better not be holding my breath.

You are wholly and fully a product of the choices you have made. I say this with the temperament of a loving parent because I know the sooner you come to this realization, the happier your life can be. When you put stock in yourself, the more joyous you will become. Blame is only a veil to hide behind. To blame is to render yourself powerless and give away the control you have over your "self." Are you a person who feels that much of what happens in your life is fate or chance? Or, are you a person who knows that life depends on your choices? The people with power in their life understand they have free will and subsequently make their life happen as they "will." They are making choices that shape their lives in a positive direction and toward a greater end and constantly reevaluating themselves and their lives to see why successes and failures occur and how to repeat the successes and turn the failures into winning experiences.

You can have the quality of life you desire so long as you choose to be responsible for it and take corresponding action. If ever you don't like the predicament in which you find yourself, don't remain in it for one more moment. Let go of any blame and anger toward others and of the belief that life is determined by people and events outside of us. It is not the hand that's been dealt to you, it's the choices you've made as the dealer.

Most of my life's accomplishments, successes, and joys I never saw coming. Maybe because I wasn't paying attention. Before most major life shifts, if you'd have asked me if they were even possible, even six months before, I would have called it madness. Me, a bodybuilder? Never. Me, musician? Are you joking? An author? Pure madness. It was a joyous ride but that's the point—I felt as though I was on a ride—a ride of which I wasn't in control. What I have come to learn in these past three decades is that I had been creating it all along. Now that I am consciously aware of this, I know I can control the ride; that I am in the driver's seat. It's much more fun this way, to know that I get to create my life through my thoughts, focus, and actions. I get to design my life and take full responsibility at the same time.

In relationship to the five habits, what is your truth? Where do you need to begin?

..............................................................................................................................................................

..............................................................................................................................................................

..............................................................................................................................................................

# UNDERSTAND THE POWER OF THE MOMENT

*This is all to say that this moment is all we have.*

Eckhart Tolle

In a moment, a life can change. In fact, the moment is all we really have. The past has already been lived in, and all we can do about the future is plan for it. It is in these moments of decision and action that your destiny and life are created. When you are writing goals, creating action plans, or deciding what immediate action you are going to take toward a particular end, you are using your personal power to move toward a better life. When you are practicing gratitude through journaling or visualizing, or mining your day for gratitude, you are using the moment to purposefully decide to feel differently. If you are in the middle of an upsetting situation and decide in the moment to get grateful—for something; anything—so you can rise above the situation and feel differently, you are using that moment of gratitude for your betterment. If you finally reach a point where you've had enough of living a sedentary life and decide that not another day shall pass without some physical activity or formal exercise, you are creating a more healthful and dynamic existence. If you are living in a typical teacher life that is full of unrelenting stress and decide to change your perspective, you are using that moment to create a transformational change. Maybe it happens through practicing mindfulness or learning how to meditate, but it is the moment of decision that moves you through this process. Never underestimate your greatest of personal powers and that is the decision to act, to physically create your life through the process of bringing your thoughts to fruition through action. The more you take advantage of every moment, to lean in and decide, the more your life can transition right before your eyes. If you had a choice to enter every day with joy, gratitude, and well-being, wouldn't you, do it?

What decision are you willing to make right now?

..................................................................................................................................

..................................................................................................................................

..................................................................................................................................

# CREATE A PLAN

*If you don't know where you are going, you'll end up someplace else.*

Yogi Berra

A bit funny, but truer words have never been spoken. If you simply want to improve one thing about daily living, a plan is necessary. Rarely do things come together without some sort of vision. I take pride in having created a life that brings me contentment and happiness. I make no judgments about anyone else's life because everyone has a different idea about life satisfaction. I have set up a life that works for me, and I have made a conscious decision to work on it every day. At fifty-five, this takes as much planning as it ever has. I'm also very open about my own triumphs and failures. My hope is that it can help someone else. I'm proud to say that, in large part, I've moved past really giving much thought to what someone else may think of me or my life, but that wasn't always the case. I'm also happy to report that age and experience brings with it perspective.

*I'd like to share a recent life experience. My version of a great life had always been college, career, marriage, home, family, friends, travel, experiences, and so on. But I woke up one day in the not-too-distant past feeling uneasy, unsettled, and not sure what to do about it. Here I was in my mid-fifties, both of my parents had died over the past five years, my kids were living their adult lives in other parts of the country, and my wife and I recently had to put down our spoiled, wonderful cockapoo of almost seventeen years. Rex was with us since the kids were in first grade. It was truly one of the worst days of my life. It was a lot of loss in a short period of time. I started thinking things like:*

"How did I get here?"

"No one prepared me for this."

"You go to college, get a degree, get married, have a family, build a career, and then one day life seemed to have bypassed me"

The biggest thing on my mind was simply this, "Now what?"

We had been busy raising twins, taking care of parents, and building careers. I now had more time on my hands than ever. How was I going to handle this? For answers, I looked at the five habits and what role they were playing in my life. Aside from getting crazily grateful for everything I already had, I needed a plan. I knew it was critical to keep wonder and joy alive and burning. I also have learned enough to know that the best time to plan the next five years of my life is now. I created a plan that included being physical every day either with my wife or friends. This helped to sustain my mental, physical, and social health. Professionally, I created a plan to contact everyone I had ever worked for to offer my professional development services. The pandemic changed how and when I offered my services. I wanted to bring some normalcy back to my work, so I wanted to get back in the room with people. This led to finding new contacts and schools to work for. We have regular social events planned on our calendar and make it a priority to spend as much time with our kids as we can. This was all part of the planning process. The most important thing I did during this time was to make the decision to contact my editor at Corwin and discuss possible interest in and next steps for this book. Obviously, by the time you read this, it has both been published and accompanied by a new business strategy and plan. Please visit thepeakperformingteacher.com for more details. As much as I want this book and business to change lives, I created them both for me. My survival and happiness depended on it.

To recap, I had a problem. Instead of letting it consume me, and I did wallow in it for a while, I used the tools and techniques I've laid out in this book to move forward. It's no joke. This is our life! If you want to live life at the highest levels and change other people's lives in the process, you need a plan. Would you ever go into your classroom without a plan? No way. Why wouldn't you do the same for your life? You have a choice. You can either wander through life being pulled along by varying forces and influences, or you can take control and be the most powerful influence in your own life through planning the next part of your life now!

What are the major things you want to plan for over the next three to five years?

..........................................................................................................................................

..........................................................................................................................................

..........................................................................................................................................

# CHANGE YOUR LIMITING BELIEFS

*Don't limit yourself. Many people limit themselves to what they think they can do. You can go as far as your mind lets you. What you believe, remember, you can achieve.*

Mary Kay Ash

I make use of visualization to help create a life without limitation. It affects everything I do. Why put limitations on myself? If no one else has ever done so, I'm giving you permission today to go after the life you want without limit. I haven't achieved everything I've set out to do. Sometimes I've simply failed, and other times my desires changed, but I always set the bar high! At times though, I've dealt with defeating and limiting self-talk that I had to grow past. When I first began teaching graduate courses I remember thinking specifically:

"Who am I to be teaching these courses?"

"Am I really the expert in the room?"

"Is my knowledge base strong enough to be of value to my audience?"

"Can I facilitate instruction in front of adults who in some cases are older and more experienced in education than I was?"

When I could have been saying to myself . . .

"I have been trained effectively and worked extremely hard to earn the right to be in this position. I have a strong background in this particular area and have stayed on top of the research to make sure I can make a difference in these teachers' lives."

The same thing happened when I coauthored my first book, *The Kinesthetic Classroom: Teaching and Learning Through Movement*. I thought at times "Who am I to write this book?" Of course, I have much more life experience now and know not to put limits on myself. I truly believe that I can do anything I set my sights on.

Sometimes people will limit themselves because of risk—risk of not being good enough, risk of failure, or risk of judgment. My answer to this is to focus on a time in your life where you took a large risk and it paid off handsomely. We want to recognize risk not as a negative but as a positive. If a risk doesn't pay off, it is not a loss but a lesson. There is risk involved in any decision we make, it's just that some risk seems more tolerable than others to the point that we forget there is risk involved at all. Taking risks is like lifting emotional weights. Every day you get stronger and stronger, and the weightlifting, or the risk-taking, gets easier and easier. I've not only taken some very significant risks, but most of them have paid off handsomely. Realizing this has made hard decisions easier to manage. My instincts usually tell me what is right even if it seems uncomfortable in the moment.

We all have taken risks, but our culture does not label them as such. Take marriage, for instance. Isn't getting married a huge risk? You barely know this person, and you could spend the next seventy years with them! For some, this risk pays back rewards through love, companionship, family, children, and so on. For others, the risk doesn't turn out so well, but they are willing to take the same risk again and again because of the possible rewards.

To date, the biggest risk I've ever taken was moving two thousand miles away from home. I was twenty-three years old and very close to my family. When I look back, I sometimes still can't believe I did that. I'm not sure where the courage came from. It was a tremendous leap of faith, and the rewards of that decision still play out for me. I found out more about myself than I ever knew, mostly that I could take care of myself and thrive. I found a group of wonderful friends who I cherish to this day. We bonded and took care of each other. I earned a master's degree and became an accomplished musician. I traveled, loved, succeeded, and failed, but lived more than I ever had up to that point. Everything would have been different had I not taken a risk and made that decision. That move also started me on my career path. I wrote my first book at the age of twenty-eight. It was never published and still sits in a filing cabinet, but it was a foreshadowing of things to come.

Now, when I look back over the major risks in my life, whether it was changing careers, becoming a public speaker, or even writing this book, I realize that it has mostly all paid off. I have no reason to fear risk. Do you?

If you could change one limiting belief, what would it be?

.........................................................................................................................................

.........................................................................................................................................

.........................................................................................................................................

## ENJOY THE PROCESS

*The prize is in the process.*

*Baron Baptiste*

What would life be if we only felt moments of joy when we reached our goals? If you don't dig into the process and get joy from every step along the way you are missing out on the opportunity for so much emotional fulfillment. There is great joy to be found in moving through the steps of your plan, noticing whether it is working or not, making adjustments to the plan if needed, and moving forward in a different way. There are so many moments to breathe in during your life. Don't get caught up in getting to the point where you've achieved your goal and say, "Now what?" Or, "Is this all there is?"

The moment I crossed the finish line at the Broad Street Run was one that I will cherish forever, but I also celebrate every step of every mile over the four-month period it took to get me to that point. If I don't, I've just narrowed my enjoyment of the process to a very small window. I want more emotional satisfaction than that! That means I must take in what surrounds me in each moment and make the most of it; that I try to find satisfaction in the very successful moments but also in the challenging ones, too. I recently heard someone say that they decided to make a conscious effort to view their pandemic year of teaching as "win or learn." What a great perspective! Life is going to happen. A process will occur. Things keep moving forward. You get to decide whether or not to recognize this and enjoy it as it comes. Don't fall into the trap of . . . "I'll be happy when (you fill in the blank)." Happiness should not be reserved only for life's achievements or completion of a goal.

Was there a time in your life that you missed out on the fulfillment of enjoying the process?

..............................................................................................................................................

..............................................................................................................................................

..............................................................................................................................................

## START NOW

*A year from now you may wish you had started today.*

Karen Lamb

There's no time like the present, right? See "Understand the power of the moment." In this moment you can decide to do whatever needs to be done. Whatever "it" is it represents a decision. Maybe you need to . . .

Create a personal mission statement

Set a goal

Learn to meditate

Make a call

Send an email

Make an inquiry

Create an action plan

Find a friend to help

Go for a walk

Go to the gym

Do it now because you are looking to create momentum! With one action can come another. Things start building on things. Successes start building on successes. Moments turn into minutes, which turn into hours, which turn into days. The idea is to begin in order to get a little bit better every day. Build the muscles of habit so they get stronger and stronger. Turn your "shoulds" into "musts!" One year from now, you'll be able to look back at all the progress you've made because of the simple decision to start now!

What "should" can you turn into a "must" right now? What action can you take immediately?

..............................................................................................................................................

..............................................................................................................................................

..............................................................................................................................................

# SURROUND YOURSELF WITH SUCCESS AND POSITIVITY

*The quality of a person's life is most often a direct reflection of the expectations of their peer group.*

Tony Robbins

I actually reflect upon, and share, this Tony Robbins quote quite regularly. It gets right to the heart of things. I have been fortunate to be surrounded by high achievers all my life, whether family or friends. They care about their health, finances, families, businesses, careers, and contributions to others. Those who I surround myself with consistently have several things in common:

1. They are committed to living their best life.

2. They are hard workers who are willing to put the necessary time in to be successful.

3. They have high expectations for themselves and for those around them.

4. They often stretch themselves beyond their comfort zones.

5. They are high achievers who take pride in almost every aspect of their lives.

These commonalities obviously rub off on me. I don't want to be the one that doesn't take care of those same things. It creates a good pressure, which I gladly accept. The standards are high, and I want to live up to them. It has been a driving force for me. Who do you surround yourself with? Who do you spend the most time with? I'm not suggesting that every friend, relative, and professional associate should have higher standards than you. It is worth your time, though, to reflect upon who comprises your inner-most circle. It's an important factor that can, in part, determine how your life will unfold. Do the individuals who surround you talk positively of others, especially students and parents? Are they positive individuals, or do they complain every chance they get? Do they engage in activities away from school that bring health and balance to their life? Are they giving people who spend time looking for ways to make life better for others?

One part of living powerfully begins with being and staying positive. It is essential to enjoying the quality in your life. The effect of every event is only determined by the meaning you place upon it. It may take practice identifying that particular aspect of truth, but when you do, you will marvel at its implications. There is no situation without some positive aspect to it. I can almost hear your thoughts. There's not much grand about losing your job, stumbling through a divorce, or suddenly becoming physically disabled. But there is something positive there for you to hold onto always, even in the most seemingly dire circumstances.

Life constantly demands choices, and you actually choose to feel a certain way about every event. You choose whether a situation is in control of you or whether you are in control of it. It is all about the judgment you make. Those who choose an optimistic and positive attitude keep their base of power intact, while those who choose a negative and pessimistic route give away their power. Is the glass half empty or half full? The answer you come up with to that simple question will change the dynamics of who you are or choose to become. It means ease, grace, and good health as opposed to despair, hopelessness, and misery. I mentioned earlier how I feel I'm living a blessed life. Someone else might have a different perspective on my life—the death of my parents, our empty nest, my three surgeries over the past five years, my bad mountain biking accident, or my contracting Covid, all adding up to overwhelming misery. Perspective is powerful.

Having a positive perspective will make you feel good. By embracing and maintaining a positive attitude you will notice a spring in your step, an internal calmness, and a new level of energy as you begin developing a new and refreshing way of looking at life. This means living positively, not just choosing certain situations to be positive about. Some people easily fool themselves into thinking they exist in a positive way. At the first sign of trouble, they sprint back to the old but comfortable negative habits of resolving life's issues.

To truly make a change in attitude you need to become aware of your internal thought processes. Are they helpful, joyous, expansive, loving, and positive, or negative and judgmental? Examine your words. How often "can't you stand something" or use the word "hate" about the most trivial of things? This applies to others around you. I'll bet some of the people in your life that you love, admire, and respect, talk more negatively than you ever realized. We have a tendency to confuse nice with positive. The next time you have the opportunity, be objective and listen carefully. Become aware of the words and statements of the company you keep. I have heard the nicest people live by and repeatedly say that if something can go wrong it probably will, because that's just the way it is. This doesn't have to be for you. Your deeply ingrained belief systems make you who you are, and it sometimes takes real soul searching and determination to make some in-depth changes. However, the rewards are great.

Positive thinkers at least give themselves a chance. They are willing to look at a situation from a different angle, learn from it, make changes, and then move on to something greater. Surround yourself with these types of individuals. They will lift you up and make you feel good. Remember, outlooks are contagious. At first, it may seem abrasive to join a crowd of positive choosing people. Their attitudes may rub you the wrong way. Life is so much more enjoyable when you greet it with a smile instead of a frown. You may need to make some difficult choices about the people with whom you spend lots of time. If they drag you down and entice you into complaining, gossiping, and bickering, then you may need to seek other company if only until you become strong enough to affect their lives with positive energy instead of letting them affect yours. I consider myself to be a positive person, but every now and again, I allow myself to get lured into a negative conversation. I find myself complaining agreeably with the person speaking. Usually, I walk away chastising myself for becoming a participant. Negativity is powerful and so common that you must be strong of will and heart to be immune to its draining energy.

I believe our destiny is knowing joy. It's what we are inherently programmed for. We are meant to soar, not crash and burn, and we are already armed with the necessary skills to accomplish these wonderful things. We need only to remember to use them. The power in your life is within. Don't think negative experiences into your life. Thoughts are powerful and in large part control your life. It is from thought that our experiences take shape, and if your thoughts are largely negative, you can bet there is trouble ahead. Becoming aware of your thought patterns will enable you to change your self-talk. When you've made progress with a smile, positive people and positive experiences will follow.

Positive people are good for our world and earth. They bring happiness and joy to themselves and others. They are infectious to the people who wish to be infected with something good. They are dynamic beings who are in control of their lives and know they retain power for themselves. They attract the good, the peaceful and the harmonious, and contribute to it as well. Positive people are like relaxing tonics. Have you ever been in the company of a joyfully positive person and found the tension in your body soothingly evaporate? Compare this to the complaining negativity of others.

Don't we all desire circumstances for a better life?? Wouldn't we all like for crucial events to go smoother? Or day-to-day living, easier? Wouldn't you hope for that? One way that can happen is through changing your perception of all that makes up your life, which involves a shift in thinking. Looking at the glass half full or half empty seems a little different than looking at the bank account as half full or half empty, but they are essentially about making the same choice. It is about recognizing the same old and tired negative patterns and choosing a new and different path. Not only will you feel better about the world around you, but you will actually begin to see change in your life. You will begin attracting positive and enriching people into your sphere, and your life can become more pleasant to be in. You will find that things that mattered before and maybe caused you grief will become a great deal less essential or even unimportant. Eventually, any type of negative person, conversation, or event will repel you. Just your presence will have a pleasing and profound effect on other lives you touch, including your students. In turn, it can also improve the quality of your own life as well. Can you afford to wait another minute?

## A FINAL WORD

It is my sincere hope that somewhere in these pages you have found inspiration that will help raise your level of living in order to serve both you and your students at the highest level possible. Both of you deserve nothing less than the very best you have to give each and every day. Focusing on the five habits can help create that path. I wish you the very best as you take the next steps!

# REFERENCES

Brandt, A. (2018, July). Science proves that gratitude is key to well-being. *Psychology Today*. https://www.psychologytoday.com/us/blog/mindful-anger/201807/science-proves-gratitude-is-key-well-being

Bryan, J. L., Young, C. M., Lucas, S., & Quist, M. C. (2018). Should I say thank you? Gratitude encourages cognitive reappraisal and buffers the negative impact of ambivalence over emotional expression on depression. *Personality and Individual Differences, 120,* 253–258. https://doi.org/10.1016/j.paid.2016.12.013

Campbell, C. (2017). How teaching gratitude in school makes kids happier. *Huffington Post*. https://www.huffpost.com/entry/how-gratitude-affects-kid_n_4310927

Canfield, J. (2005). *The success principles*. HarperCollins.

Chowdhury, M. (2021). The science and psychology of goal-setting 101. *PositivePsychology.com*. https://positivepsychology.com/goal-setting-psychology/

Cousins, N. (1979). *Anatomy of an illness as perceived by the patient*. W.W. Norton & Company.

Covey, S. R. (2004) *The 7 habits of highly effective people*. Simon & Schuster.

Craig, H. (2021). The research on gratitude and its link with love and happiness. *Positivepsychology.com*. https://positivepsychology.com/gratitude-research/

Cuddy, A. (2012). Your body language may shape who you are. *TED Talk*. https://www.youtube.com/watch?v=Ks-_Mh1QhMc&t=9s

Daghlas, I., Lane, J., Saxena, R., & Vetter, C. (2021). Genetically proxied diurnal preference, sleep timing, and risk of major depressive disorder. *JAMA Psychiatry*. https://pubmed.ncbi.nlm.nih.gov/34037671/

Dalio, R. (2017). *Principles*. Simon & Schuster.

Davis, D., & Hayes, J. (2012, July/August). What are the benefits of mindfulness? *American Psychological Association, 43*(7). https://www.apa.org/monitor/2012/07-08/ce-corner

Ebert, J. (2005). A broken heart harms your health. *Nature*. https://doi.org/10.1038/news050207-11

Ekelund, U., Tarp, J., Fagerland, M. W., Johannessen, J. S., Hansen, B. H., Jefferis, B., Whincup, P., Diaz, K., Hooker, S., Howard, V., Chernofsky, A., Larson, M., Spartano, N., Vasan, R., Dohrn, I., Hagströmer, M., Edwardson, C., Yates, T., Shiroma, E., Dempsey, P., Wijndaele, K., Anderssen, S., Lee, I. (2020). Joint associations of accelerometer-measured physical activity and sedentary time with all-cause mortality: a harmonised meta-analysis in more than 44 000 middle-aged and older individuals. *British Journal of Sports Medicine, 54,* 1499–1506.

Fahey, R. (2020). *Your best decade*. Tellwell.

Fisher, M. (2020). 7 ways exercise makes you happy—and how much you need to improve your mood. *Insider*. https://www.insider.com/does-exercise-make-you-happy

Froh, J., & Bono, G. (2012, November). How to foster gratitude in schools. *Greater Good Magazine*. https://greatergood.berkeley.edu/article/item/how_to_foster_gratitude_in_schools

Froh, J., Emmons, R., Card, N., Bono, G., & Wilson, J. (2011). Gratitude and the reduced costs of materialism in adolescents. *Journal of Happiness Studies, 12*(2), 289–302.

Froh, J., Sefick, W., & Emmons, R., (2008). Counting blessings in early adolescents: An experimental study of gratitude and subjective well-being. *Journal of School Psychology, 46,* 213–233 (PDF, 410KB).

Hanh, N. (1987). *The Miracle of Mindfulness*. Beacon Press.

Hardisty, D., & Weber, E. (2020). Impatience and savoring vs. dread: Asymmetries in anticipation explain consumer time preferences for positive vs. negative events. *Journal of Consumer Psychology*. https://myscp.onlinelibrary.wiley.com/doi/full/10.1002/jcpy.1169

Hwang, W. (2016). *Culturally adapting psychotherapy for Asian heritage populations*. Academic Press.

Howells, K. (2013). How thanking awakens our thinking. *TEDx Talk*. https://www.youtube.com/watch?v=gzfhPB_NtVc&t=190s

Klein, H. J., Lount, R. B., Jr., Park, H. M., & Linford, B. J. (2020). When goals are known: The effects of audience relative status on goal commitment and performance. *Journal of Applied Psychology, 105*(4), 372–389. https://doi.org/10.1037/apl0000441

Lally, P., van Jaarsveld, C., Potts, H., & Wardle, J. (2009). How are habits formed: Modeling habits formation in the real world. *European Journal of Social Psychology, 40*(6), 998–1009.

Lance, J. (2019, April). 7 Science-backed secrets of a productive morning routine. https://positiveroutines.com/productive-morning-routine/

Langer, E. J. (2016). *The power of mindful learning*. Da Capo Press.

Lengel, T., & Kuczala, M. (2010). *The kinesthetic classroom: Teaching and learning through Movement*. Corwin.

Lindsey, J. (2019). Do this in the morning for a better workday. *Greater Good Magazine*. https://greatergood.berkeley.edu/article/item/do_this_in_the_morning_for_a_better_workday

Ma, M., Kibler, J., & Sly, K. (2013). Gratitude is associated with greater levels of protective factors and lower levels of risks in African American adolescents. *Journal of Adolescence, 36*(5), 983–991.

Mayo Clinic. (2016, April 16). *Stress relief from laughter? It's no joke*. Healthy Lifestyle. Retrieved November 24, 2017, from https://www.mayoclinic.org/healthy-lifestyle/stress-management/in-depth/stress-relief/art-20044456

McGuey, G., & Moore, L. (2007). *The inspirational teacher*. Eye on Education.

More evidence that exercise can boost mood. (2019, May). Harvard Health Publishing. https://www.health.harvard.edu/mind-and-mood/more-evidence-that-exercise-can-boost-mood

Morin, A. (2014, November). 7 Scientifically proven benefits of gratitude that will motivate you to give thanks year-round. *Forbes*. https://www.forbes.com/sites/amymorin/2014/11/23/7-scientifically-proven-benefits-of-gratitude-that-will-motivate-you-to-give-thanks-year-round/?sh=44739251183c

Morin, A. (2021, July). What is cognitive reframing? *Very Well Mind*. https://www.verywellmind.com/reframing-defined-2610419

Moses, V. (2021). A non-randomizd study investigating the effectiveness of cognitive reframing in socially disconnected widows. *The European Research Journal, 7*(1), 1–11.

Mukherjee, M., Ramirez, R., & Cuthbertson, R. (February 2, 2016). Scenarios research and cognitive reframing: Implications for strategy as practice. Saïd Business School WP 2016-07, Available at SSRN: https://ssrn.com/abstract=2729827

Neihart, M. (2008). *Peak performance for smart kids*. Prufrock Press.

Nordengren, C. (2019). Goal-setting practices that support a learning culture. *Phi Delta Kappan*. https://kappanonline.org/goal-setting-practices-support-learning-culture-nordengren/

Palta, P., Sharrett, A. R., Gabriel, K. P., Gottesman, R. F., Folsom, A. R., Power, M. C., Evenson, K. R., Jack, C. R., Knopman, D. S., Mosley, T. H., & Heiss, G. (2021). Prospective analysis of leisure-time physical activity in midlife and beyond and brain damage on MRI in older adults. *Neurology, 96*(7), e964–e974.

Price-Mitchell, M. (2018). Goal-setting is linked to higher achievement. *Psychology Today*. https://www.psychologytoday.com/us/blog/the-moment-youth/201803/goal-setting-is-linked-higher-achievement

Ramakrishnan, R., Doherty, A., Smith-Byrne, K., Rahimi, K., Bennett, D., Woodward, M. Walmsley, R., & Dwyer, T. (2021). Accelerometer measured physical activity and the incidence of cardiovascular disease: Evidence from the UK Biobank cohort study. *PLoS Medicine, 18*(1), e1003487. https://doi.org/10.1371/journal.pmed.1003487

Randler, C. (2010). *Defend your research: The early bird really does get the worm*. Harvard Business Review. https://hbr.org/2010/07/defend-your-research-the-early-bird-really-does-get-the-worm

Ratey, J. (2008). *SPARK: The revolutionary new science of exercise and the brain.* Little, Brown & Company.

Research related to gratitude. https://gratefulness.org/resource/research-related-to-gratitude/

Robbins, A. (1991). *Awaken the giant within.* Simon & Schuster.

Robbins, T. (2014). *Money: Master the game.* Simon & Schuster.

Rothbard, N., & Wilk, S. (2011). Waking up on the right side of the bed: Start-of-workday mood, work events, employee affect, and performance. *Academy of Management Journal, 54*(5), 969–980.

Sansone, R. A., & Sansone, L. (2010, November). Gratitude and well being: The benefits of appreciation. *Psychiatry, 7*(11), 18–22. https://www.ncbi.nlm.nih.gov/pmc/articles/PMC3010965/

Sheldon, K. M., & Lyubomirsky, S. (2006). How to increase and sustain positive emotion: The effects of expressing gratitude and visualizing best possible selves. *The Journal of Positive Psychology, 1*(2), 73–82. https://doi.org/10.1080/17439760500510676

Sonnentag, S., Eck, K., & Fritz, C. (2019). Morning reattachment to work and work engagement during the day: A look at day-level mediators. *Journal of Management, 46*(8), 1408–1435.

Sousa, D. (2017). *How the brain learns.* Corwin.

Steindl-Rast, D. (2013). Want to be happy? Be grateful. *TED Talk.* https://www.youtube.com/watch?v=UtBsl3j0YRQ&t=58s

Thorpe, M., & Link, R. (2020, October). 12 science-based benefits of meditation. *Healthline.* https://www.healthline.com/nutrition/12-benefits-of-meditation

Tubesing, N., & Tubesing, D. A. (Eds.). (1983). Group energizers. In *Structured exercises in stress management: A whole person handbook for trainers, educators, and group leaders, Volume 1* (p. 116). Whole Person Press.

Usher, A., & Kober, N. (2012). *Student motivation: An overlooked piece of school reform.* Center for Education Policy.

von Sonnenberg, E. (2011). Ready, set, goals! *Positive Psychology News.* https://positivepsychologynews.com/news/emily-vansonnenberg/2011010315821

Walton, A. (2015, February). 7 ways meditation can actually change the brain. *Forbes.* https://www.forbes.com/sites/alicegwalton/2015/02/09/7-ways-meditation-can-actually-change-the-brain/?sh=437ccb0b1465

# INDEX

A SAGE Publishing Company

# Keep learning...

## Also from Mike Kuczala

### READY, SET, GO!

### The Kinesthetic Classroom 2.0

Kinesthetic education is your answer to brain-friendly motivation and learning! Discover hundreds of practical, easy-to-implement activities and movements that rev up your teaching and spark optimal learning. This 4-part framework of activities promotes an energized learning environment where mental and emotional growth is met with physical, social, and cognitive engagement.

### THE KINESTHETIC CLASSROOM

### Teaching and Learning Through Movement

Drawing on cutting-edge educational research, this book describes how regular physical movement improves attention span and helps the brain master new information. Learn how to use specific physical activities to prepare the brain to learn, engage the academic curriculum, and enhance student motivation.

## Professional Development Workshops

**Mike Kuczala** is a bestselling author, acclaimed keynote speaker, and innovative professional developer. He is dedicated to working with your school or district to custom-create the most memorable professional development your educational staff has ever experienced.

Please visit mikekuczala.com and thepeakperformingteacher.com for information about professional development.

TMN21C32